"Society is no friend to the teenager, but Gwen Diaz has befriended young people by clearly explaining that 'identity' is determined by who we let God be inside of us. Using John 13 as a launching pad, the book treats ten core issues that teens deal with on a regular basis. The chapter on 'anger' alone makes the book worth reading."

— Harry E. Walker, chairman, Bible department at
Black Forest Academy, Kandern, Germany

STICKING UP FOR WHO I AM

Answers to the *Emotional* Issues Teenagers Raise

Gwendolyn Mitchell Diaz

BRINGING TRUTH TO LIFE
P.O. Box 35001, Colorado Springs, Colorado 80935

Our Guarantee to You

We believe so strongly in the message of our books that we are making this quality guarantee to you. If for any reason you are disappointed with the content of this book, return the title page to us with your name and address and we will refund to you the list price of the book. To help us serve you better, please briefly describe why you were disappointed. Mail your refund request to: NavPress, P.O. Box 35002, Colorado Springs, CO 80935.

The Navigators is an international Christian organization. Our mission is to reach, disciple, and equip people to know Christ and to make Him known through successive generations. We envision multitudes of diverse people in the United States and every other nation who have a passionate love for Christ, live a lifestyle of sharing Christ's love, and multiply spiritual laborers among those without Christ.

NavPress is the publishing ministry of The Navigators. NavPress publications help believers learn biblical truth and apply what they learn to their lives and ministries. Our mission is to stimulate spiritual formation among our readers.

ISBN 1-57683-310-0

Cover design by Ray Moore
Cover photo from Creasource/Picture Quest
Creative Team: Paul Santhouse, Greg Clouse, Darla Hightower, Glynese Northam

Some of the anecdotal illustrations in this book are true to life and are included with the permission of the persons involved. All other illustrations are composites of real situations, and any resemblance to people living or dead is coincidental.

Library of Congress Cataloging-in-Publication Data

Diaz, Gwendolyn Mitchell.
Sticking up for who I am : answers to the emotional issues teenagers raise / Gwendolyn Mitchell Diaz.
p. cm.
Includes bibliographical references.
ISBN 1-57683-310-0
1. Emotions in adolescence. 2. Emotions in adolescence--Religious aspects--Christianity. 3. Teenagers--Religious life. I. Title.
BF724.3.E5 D53 2003
248.8'3--dc21

2002151983

Printed in the United States of America

1 2 3 4 5 6 7 8 9 10 / 07 06 05 04 03

DEAR PARENT,

This book is the third in a series based on discussions with my four sons: Zachary, Matthew, Benjamin, and Jonathan. It was written to help them get a handle on the feelings and emotions that tend to influence a teenager's outlook on life. Like the first two (*Sticking Up for What I Believe* and *Sticking Up for What Is Right*), it was originally written just for them based on the experiences that we shared together. Now they are allowing me to share it with you.

I challenge you to read it yourself to better grasp the emotional dilemmas that affect your teens and pre-teens; borrow the ideas and fill in your own stories to share at appropriate moments; or loan it to your kids to read by themselves. There is no better place to honestly confront the emotional issues that challenge our teenagers than in the home. However, when questions arise that require further counsel, I would urge you to obtain the help of a professional who seeks wisdom from the Word of God.

GWENDOLYN MITCHELL DIAZ

CONTENTS

ACKNOWLEDGMENTS

To Kent Wilson and Paul Santhouse,

Thank you for the excitement you brought to this project from the very beginning and the insights you shared along the way. Your encouragement meant a lot to me!

To Greg Clouse and Darla Hightower,

These books would not exist without your wisdom and expertise. Thank you for being such discerning and kind editors! It is a tremendous privilege to work with you!

To Dr. Paul Suich,

The knowledge and insights you shared with me greatly enriched my understanding of emotional issues. Thank you (and Cynthia) for being such great friends and cheerleaders.

To Terry Frost, Cindy Cleveland, Jessica Hart, and Susan McCaskill,

I treasured your prayers every step of the way!

And to my family,

I could not have prepared these three books for publication without your loving help! Thank you for putting up with all my questions and allowing me to share so many of our "secrets" with others. I am grateful for all the times you were willing to eat burgers, do the laundry, and put up with grunge in the shower so that I could work on manuscripts. ILYUTTS!

INTRODUCTION

How Can I Stick Up for *Someone I Don't Even Know?*

What's the first thing you check out when you walk past a store window at the mall? Is it the latest fashions or fads for the new season; or the new look in mannequins; or the colors and designs used in the display cases?

Be honest now. It's none of the above, is it? I know that the first thing I check out when I walk past a store window is my own reflection — and I'm willing to bet that you give yours more than just a passing glance. Am I right? You want to see how you look — especially compared with everyone else at the mall. You want to see if your sweater is baggy enough, or if it's too baggy and needs to be tucked under a little more at the bottom. You want to know if you should push the sleeves up past your elbows or leave them flopping down over your wrists. How about your hair? You want to know if it's okay, or if it's really as bad as you thought it was before you left home. You look down at your feet and you're ticked because you didn't escape from the house before I made you put on a "decent pair of shoes." Flip-flops would have been so much more comfortable and cool-looking, even though it's only thirty degrees outside.

More than likely the reason you and I stand there evaluating every aspect of how we look, while pretending to check out the latest T-shirt logos, has nothing to do with being stuck on ourselves. It has everything to do with being a little insecure. We're trying to figure out exactly who we really are. We're afraid that the image we put together before heading to the mall might not be the right one for the occasion. We're not sure if we measure up to everyone else's expectations. We know for certain that we don't measure up to our own desires.

One day several years ago I went out shopping all by myself. (Obviously I don't get to do that very often, since I remember this one incident so vividly.) None of you were along to drag me into the electronics store; or to try to coax me into buying you a new CD; or to lure me into checking out the puppies at the pet shop. No one was begging for the latest pair of running shoes or zooming off down the concourse to buy frozen yogurt. You were all off doing your own thing, and Dad was home watching a football playoff game.

As I walked by the stationery store, I caught a glimpse of myself in the window. What a shock! Without the usual props — a stroller and four little guys hanging all over me — I looked pretty pathetic. Surely I hadn't become the woman I saw staring back at me. I had to be a lot younger and shapelier than that!

I looked around at how other women were dressed and realized that I was definitely in need of a wardrobe lift! Wants and desires that I had not allowed myself to entertain for years began to accompany me as I strolled down the long mall corridor, and soon I found myself entering a trendy little dress "shoppe" with gray-skinned, no-eyed, alien-looking mannequins.

I don't know what possessed me, but for some reason I tried on a pair of neon stretch pants with a matching over-sized T-shirt. I had noticed several chic ladies at the food court wearing similar outfits. When I peered into the three-way mirror, I was thrilled with the sophisticated, maybe even alluring, lady staring back at me. She cocked her head back as if she were a model posing in front of a row of cameras. She preened and poked at her hair like teenagers do when they are standing in line at the movie theater.

She looked very nice — at least according to the sales lady, who easily talked her into buying a matching pair of socks, some dangly earrings, and a sash that would "bring the whole outfit together." And at that point she looked "just darling."

All she needed was a huge, shiny clip to sweep her hair up on top of her head, the sales lady insisted. (Who was I to argue?)

As soon as I got home I put on the outfit, so excited about my new look that I decided to impress you all right away. I even took extra time to sweep my hair up on top of my head with my funky new clip.

First I modeled the whole ensemble for Dad. "That's really . . . different," he said without wasting much enthusiasm or charm. (I'm sure he was trying very hard not to say anything that would get him in trouble during the middle of the play-off season.) I decided to ignore him, because he doesn't know anything about fashion anyway, and I strolled into the family room.

"How do you like my new outfit, guys?" I asked, interrupting a video game.

The four of you barely looked up. A flat "cool," a "yeah," and an "hmm" were your overwhelming responses.

"Doesn't anyone like how I look?" I asked again, insisting on being noticed. "How about my hair? Do you like it like this?"

I should have known better than to push it. Jonathan, taking upon himself the full burden of honesty and tact, was the only one who answered.

"Well, Mom," the words kind of squeezed their way out of his mouth. "That's just how you would want to wear your hair . . . if you were young enough to wear an outfit like that."

I was crushed. I didn't like the old "me" I had caught a glimpse of in the store window, and none of you liked the new "me" I had created that day. Needless to say, my self-image took a real hit. I wasn't at all sure who I was. And I hated the imposter wearing my new clothes.

That shopping trip was the beginning of a process that God took me through to teach me that *who I am* has nothing to do with what I look like or the things that I own. It isn't attached to what I can or cannot do or where I have or have not been. It isn't connected to how many people like me, or whether or not they choose to applaud my accomplishments.

Who I am is determined by who I let God be inside of me. And *His* identity never changes.

That day at the mall, I knew that there was a lot more to the real "me" than the image in the store window, but I had no idea how to convey it. It was hidden somewhere deep inside of me. And buying a new outfit didn't help bring it out in any way.

I know that you understand what I'm talking about. You've had the same experiences. You are aware of feelings and fantasies and knowledge and dreams and depths in your soul that no one has a clue you own. But how do you get in touch with all that? How can you feel worthwhile regardless of what's going on around you—regardless of what people think? And how can you control your emotions—jealousy, anger, fear, and pain—when everyone else seems to be letting theirs run rampant?

These are some of the issues I want to discuss with you. I want you to know how awesome God thinks you are and how proud He is of the way He made you. You are a one-of-a-kind masterpiece created by Him to do unbelievable things. He wants you to like the person who happens to be wearing your clothes.

ISSUE #1

So, Who Am I?

It was graduation night at Delsea Regional High School in Franklinville, New Jersey. Like every other girl, I had on a white gown, a white mortarboard (that's one of those square hats with a tassel), and white shoes. I remember being seated on an uncomfortable folding chair in the middle of a row, in the middle of a high school football field, in the middle of a bunch of faculty and dignitaries. Yet in the midst of all those people I felt alienated and lonely.

The co-valedictorians had been caught drinking on the senior trip and were graduating in a state of disgrace. They weren't allowed to make their speeches, and, much to my dismay, I had been chosen to fill in for them. Giving a speech in front of the whole world was definitely not my idea of fun.

As a matter of fact, the entire day had been pretty miserable. My father, who often became disoriented in the early stages of Alzheimer's disease, had created several disruptive situations. I had not had any time to review my speech and very little time to get dressed. And, on top of everything else, my car had run out of gas right as I crossed the railroad tracks on my way to the ceremony!

I arrived just in time to hear the band strike up the first few bars of "Pomp and Circumstance" and find my place in line. (Fortunately it was near the end.) My hair, which had spent most of the day in rollers, lay limp and stringy down my back due to the humidity and gale-force winds that preceded a brewing late-spring storm. The band didn't get very far in their song before the wind whipped the music right off their stands. So we finished our procession in silence.

After a bunch of uninspiring rhetoric, it was my turn to step to the podium. I remember thinking how stupid my speech was. I had been advised to go with an uplifting "new day, new world" theme. I heard myself saying things like, "Here we stand on the shores of a new tomorrow . . . sandy beaches spread before us . . . a new day dawning." It was a bright, rosy, challenging speech, but I knew that no one there was feeling particularly bright or rosy or like taking on any new challenges. We had just entered the Vietnam War!

As I finished talking, a gust of wind caught my manuscript and blew it off the podium, across the field, and into oblivion. I remember thinking that justice had probably been served on that useless piece of paper, and I trudged back to my seat.

I sat there in misery—wondering if everyone had hated the speech as much as I had; wondering if Joey, who had already shaved his head and was heading for basic training the next day, would ever make it home alive; wondering if I should carry out my plans to go to college, since my father was so sick; wondering what my role was in a messed-up world that was falling apart.

Just then an administrator was called forward to present the Faculty Bowl, a prize given annually to a graduating senior selected by the staff as the student they had enjoyed teaching the most. It wasn't based on GPA or sports involvement or leadership skills, although all of these somehow entered into the decision.

I knew it was going to be presented to my best friend. Everybody loved her. She lit up any classroom she walked into and got along great with everyone in the school. She earned good grades and participated in lots of activities. I was thrilled for her. She deserved it, plus she was going through some tough times of her own, and she certainly could use the accolades.

As they extolled the worth of the recipient and began to unveil her identity, I was even more convinced that it belonged to my friend. In fact, I was so sure that Karen had won the Faculty Bowl that when they announced my name, I just shook my head and remained seated.

The teacher seated next to me nudged me and said, "You have to go up front to get it. They aren't going to bring it to you."

"No," I replied. "They weren't talking about me. They said the wrong name."

She laughed and pushed me up front to receive the shiny silver bowl with my name engraved on it.

I was stunned. Over the next few days I tried to reconcile the person who I thought I was with the person who had just received the faculty's highest honor. I wondered how I could have assessed myself so differently than my teachers had. *Maybe it really was a mistake. Maybe the engraver had accidentally put my name on the trophy and the principal had made the decision to go with it because it would cost too much to make a new one.*

I wondered how differently I would have approached my high school days if I had known what I was really worth to my teachers. Maybe I would have raised my hand more often in class, realizing that I really did have something to offer. Perhaps I would have felt that my opinion held a little more value in discussions with my peers. Instead of creating excuses for why I couldn't attend drinking parties down by the lake or travel to weekend bashes at the beach, maybe I would have stood up to my friends and told them why I *really* didn't go.

In a world that seemed hostile to everything I stood for or had been raised to believe, I didn't feel that my life held any real dignity or value. I certainly didn't feel secure in who I was or the things I had accomplished or where I was headed in life.

Over the years I have discovered that most high school students wrestle with these same insecurities, but there are many different ways of responding. Some teenagers become angry or react in defiance to what causes them discomfort. Some withdraw or try to hide from potential pain. Others, like me, overachieve in order to find significance.

Almost all teenagers, at some point in time, come to the conclusion that this world is a hostile, unfriendly place. They struggle to discover their identity, strain to maintain their dignity, and strive to establish some sort of security in a world that offers little stability.

But guess what else I've discovered? *No one has to feel this way!* I want you to know that it is possible for you to feel good about who you are, delight in what you are worth, and rejoice in where you are headed — regardless of what is going on around you.

A LESSON FROM THE LIFE OF CHRIST

Do you realize that Jesus Christ had to deal with most of the same issues that we face? Actually, the challenges He had to cope with were far more severe than anything we will ever encounter. Yet He was able to function with great poise, dignity, and strength. Have you ever wondered how He did it? Let's look at one of the most difficult situations He confronted during His time here on earth and see what we can discover.

According to John 13, Jesus and His disciples were in Jerusalem preparing to celebrate the Passover feast. It was Jesus' last evening here on earth. He knew this, and many times He had tried to prepare His disciples for the upcoming events. But instead of listening to His message, they chose to debate with Him, arguing over which one of them would be the greatest in the new kingdom that they planned to help Him establish. They remained densely naive about Jesus' real purpose and plans.

As Jesus sat down to eat His Last Supper, He knew that one of the men seated across the table would soon betray Him. He realized that when He left that meal He would walk across the valley to the Garden of Gethsemane and would be handed over to the Roman guards. He was aware that He would spend the rest of that night and most of the next day in shackles, shuffled from courtyards to courtrooms to face false accusations and unlawful condemnation. He understood that all of His disciples would turn their cowardly backs on Him and that one of His closest friends would blatantly deny that he even knew Him — not once, but *three times!* Jesus knew that He would be brutally beaten and maliciously maligned. He fully comprehended the fact that before the sun set the next day He would be led to Golgotha, hung on a cross, and left to die for the sins of the world.

Yet look at what Jesus did:

> The evening meal was being served, and the devil had already prompted Judas Iscariot, son of Simon, to betray Jesus. Jesus knew that the Father had put all things under his power, and that he had come from God and was returning to God; so he got up

> from the meal, took off his outer clothing, and wrapped a towel around his waist. After that, he poured water into a basin and began to wash his disciples' feet, drying them with the towel that was wrapped around him (John 13:2-5).

Knowing all that He knew, Jesus, seated in a room filled with arrogant, argumentative disciples, got up from the table, laid aside His outward dignity, and washed their feet. How could He bring Himself to do such a menial task? How could he choose to humble Himself at such a time as this and do what only the least valuable of all servants would be expected to do? How could He so successfully accomplish what God had sent Him to do with such poise and dignity and confidence?

One phrase in the middle of this passage gives us the keys to Jesus' ability to succeed in a world that was filled with hostility and pain: "Jesus knew that the Father had put all things under his power, and that he had come from God and was returning to God" (verse 3).

JESUS UNDERSTOOD HIS AWESOME IDENTITY

Everyone in Israel knew Him as "Jesus of Nazareth." And everyone in Israel knew that Nazareth was not the greatest town in the world to be associated with. A Roman military barracks known for its boozing and brawling, it had absolutely no social prestige. As a matter of fact, when Philip ran to get his brother, Nathanael, so that he could introduce him to this man, "Jesus of Nazareth," whom he recognized as the Messiah, Nathanael responded, "Nazareth! Can anything good come from there?" (John 1:46). Nobody who was anybody would ever claim Nazareth as his hometown — most certainly not the Messiah!

But not only was Jesus looked down on because He was from *Nazareth,* He was snubbed because he had a lousy occupation. Mark 6:1-3 tells us that the people were offended that a *carpenter,* the son of Mary, the brother of James and Joseph and Judas and Simon, would try to teach them anything. Who did He think He was anyway? He belonged back in the shop making benches with His brothers.

The crowds went even further in their disdain for Jesus. They accused Him of being born out of wedlock. "Illegitimate" is how they referred to Him in John 8:41. They knew that Mary was His mother, but they weren't convinced that Joseph was His father. (They certainly didn't know who His real Father was!)

The world Jesus lived in was also hostile toward His friendships. In Luke 15:2, the Pharisees and teachers of the Law angrily accused Him of welcoming sinners and eating with them. They even accused Him of being a *friend* of sinners — an accusation, by the way, which He never denied.

Nothing Jesus was or did was good enough to please the "important" people in His society. Yet He never let His identity destroy Him. That's because Jesus knew that He wasn't really from Nazareth. He knew that He was much more than a carpenter — and the son of Mary. He knew that there was nothing illegitimate about His birth. As a matter of fact, He knew that it had been legitimized by a host of heavenly angels. And he knew that His job was to take the message of salvation to people who recognized their need regardless of their background.

Despite what anyone said about Him, Jesus understood His true identity. He had *"come from God"* (John 13:3). He knew that ultimately — beyond anything anyone else could think or say about Him or His hometown or His upbringing or His friends — He was the Son of God!

JESUS UNDERSTOOD HIS INCREDIBLE DIGNITY

According to John 13:3, Jesus also *"knew that the Father had put all things under his power."* In other words, He knew what he was worth.

"Hold on a second," you say. "Jesus wasn't worth very much at all. Judas only got thirty pieces of silver for Him when he sold Him to the Pharisees (see Matthew 27:3). And Jesus didn't even own a house or a bed or anything! (see Luke 9:58). He was totally destitute if you ask me."

Yes, by worldly standards Jesus was not worth very much at all. But in God's eyes, He was worth *everything!* Jesus had lived and ministered through thirty-some tough years here on earth, and He had one horrific day yet to spend on it. But once He completed what God had asked Him to do, He knew that every single thing was going to be placed back under His control. He knew that He was more valuable to God than everything in this universe put together. And Jesus' dignity came from what He was worth to God — not what He was worth in the society that surrounded Him.

JESUS UNDERSTOOD HIS INDESTRUCTIBLE SECURITY

Jesus was able to wash His disciples' feet that horrible evening in Jerusalem for yet another reason. He knew without any doubt where He was headed when it was over.

Oh, did you think He was going to Gethsemane to be betrayed? Did you hear me say that He was headed to the courtrooms of Jerusalem to be tried and the courtyards of the palace to be denied? Wasn't He on His way to Golgotha to be crucified?

No, these were just uncomfortable stopping places on a much longer journey — a journey that would ultimately take Him back to His real home.

Jesus knew where He was really headed — all the way to the glories of heaven. Nothing, not even an insulting death on a cruel cross, could keep Him from reuniting with His real Father. Jesus' security in life lay in the knowledge of His ultimate destination. *"He was returning to God"* (John 13:3).

You see, God had prepared His Son to survive in a hostile environment. He had equipped Him with an awesome identity, an incredible dignity, and an indestructible security. That's how Jesus was able to walk into a room filled with arrogant, argumentative disciples, lay aside all His outward dignity, and wash their feet.

AN EXAMPLE FROM "THE SPACE RACE"

Back in the 1960s, in an effort to win what the world referred to as "The Space Race," NASA was faced with the challenge of putting a man on the moon before the Russians did. Though the moon appears so pleasant in the night sky, it is a very hostile place. On the side farthest from the sun, its surface reaches temperatures hundreds of degrees too cold for human survival. And on the side closest to the sun, it reaches temperatures that would toast a man in milliseconds. Add to that a rugged terrain, decreased gravity, lack of moisture, and very little oxygen and you have an incredibly unfriendly environment!

NASA not only had to design a way to safely transport men to the surface of the moon, they had to come up with a way for their astronauts to deal with the extreme harshness of the environment once they arrived. It is possible that they could have designed an elaborate system of fans and air conditioners to reduce the temperature on the hot side. Or they might have developed elaborate heating devices to warm up the cold side. Instead, NASA outfitted each astronaut with a huge white space suit and a hippy-dippy backpack that provided him with a completely habitable temperature, plenty of moisture, and the necessary oxygen to survive in such a harsh and hostile place.

I'm sure you have seen the grainy, black-and-white pictures on TV of what happened when the crew landed. The men on that mission not only survived — they thrived! They bounded across the surface of the moon in great leaps and hops. They zoomed around in a lunar dune buggy kicking up moon dust everywhere they went. They hit golf balls into the craters and exuberantly planted an American flag on a lunar lump.

NASA chose not to change the hostile environment of the moon. Instead they chose to equip their men to deal with it. God did the same thing for His Son when He sent Him on a mission to this earth. And He does the same thing for us. God does not change the harshness or the hostility of the world in which we have to function. Instead He equips us to handle it. And just as Jesus functioned successfully and joyfully when He was here on earth, so can we.

WE HAVE AN AWESOME IDENTITY

It doesn't matter where or how or by whom we were raised, but at some time in our lives, our backgrounds will not be "good enough" for the people around us. If we were raised up North, we are considered to be Yankees, and some people in the South will automatically assume that we are rude. If we are from the South, sooner or later someone from up North will tease us for our slow pace or our heavy drawl. Regardless of the college we choose to attend, someone who graduated from somewhere else will talk smack about our education. At some point in life, we all find out that we are not rich enough or smart enough or poised enough or short-or-tall-or-thin-or-fat-or-dark-or-light enough to measure up to everyone's standards.

But where we are from, and who raised us, and what we end up doing for a living have nothing to do with who we really are, because God has given us a new identity. If we have accepted His gift of salvation through Jesus' death on the cross, *we are His children*. The Bible says, "To all who received him, to those who believed in his name, he gave the right to become children of God" (John 1:12). Isn't that incredible! We are not the products of our past positions or the sums of our present conditions. We are children of the King of the Universe. Beyond what anyone else can ever think or say about our hometowns, our upbringing, or our friends, we have an awesome identity!

WE HAVE INCREDIBLE DIGNITY

Have you ever wondered what God was thinking the day He put the details of your body together? I'll never understand why He chose to put scraggly hair and a long, skinny neck on the same person. (But one day I'm going to ask Him!) And what's up with all the freckles? The melanin machine must have malfunctioned the day I went by on the conveyor belt!

We all have feelings of inferiority that accompany our perceptions of the containers God created for us to live inside. And they often lead us to believe that we aren't very valuable to Him. Yet in Psalm 139, the psalmist explains that we are the creative handiwork of God. He was actively and intricately involved in forming every feature of our bodies when we were hidden in our mothers' wombs. And the unique body He designed for us is the only one that can perfectly handle the details of each day that He has planned for us.

> For you created my inmost being; you knit me together in my mother's womb. I praise you

> because I am fearfully and wonderfully made; your works are wonderful, I know that full well. My frame was not hidden from you when I was made in the secret place. When I was woven together in the depths of the earth, your eyes saw my unformed body. All the days ordained for me were written in your book before one of them came to be (Psalm 139:13-16).

God loves us and He designed each one of us with fabulous things in mind. His plans for us are so much more wonderful than any we could make for ourselves. Isaiah 55:8-9 tells us that as high as the heavens are from the earth, that's how much higher and better His thoughts and His plans are than any we could come up with. We are incredibly valuable to God in every detail of our being.

Have you ever seen a picture of an old-fashioned balance scale? I'm talking about the kind that the blindfolded statue of Justice holds in our courts of law. It had two sides. On one side you placed the item that you wanted to weigh. On the other side you added weights until the scale was balanced. Once you figured out how much an item weighed, you could figure out how much it was worth.

Well, your value is what someone else is willing to place on the opposite side of a theoretical balance scale from you. You can tell how much you are worth to others by the amount of time or effort or emotion they are willing to give up for you. Believe me, some days people will leave you feeling pretty worthless.

But do you know how much God was willing to place on the opposite side of the balance scale when He looked at you? He was willing to place His one and only Son on the cross to die. If you had been the only human being alive, God would still have sacrificed Jesus just so that you could be given the opportunity to choose to have a relationship with Him. Wow! That's mind-boggling value! Your true dignity comes from what you are worth to God, not what you are worth to society. In God's eyes you have incredible dignity and value — *and no one else's opinion matters at all!*

WE HAVE INDESTRUCTIBLE SECURITY

The men who designed and built the luxury liner *Titanic* claimed that it was unsinkable. But on April 14, 1912, on its maiden voyage, the *Titanic* hit an iceberg, and less than three hours later it lay on the bottom of the ocean along with over a thousand men, women, and children.

Bo Jackson was no doubt one of the most famous athletes in recent decades. He played two professional sports, and he played them very well. He was an all-star in both Major League Baseball and the National Football League. However, a hip injury prematurely sidelined him, and you probably don't even know his name.

Jim Hall from Arkansas amassed a fortune in the Alaskan gold rush, but wasted much of his wealth on wine and women. (Once he offered to buy a woman he liked for her weight in gold. She cost him over twenty thousand dollars in gold dust!) He made one wise investment when he built the Greentree Hotel in the shadow of the scar-faced mountain known as Midnight Dome in the most expensive section of Dawson, Alaska. But that investment was reduced to ashes when a dance-hall girl accidentally started a fire that burned up over half a million dollars of Dawson real estate.[1]

Kim Alexis was once proclaimed to be the most beautiful and most photographed woman in the world. Yet she admits that while she was modeling she was miserable. She constantly had to diet and often cried herself to sleep at night. She much prefers her role as wife and mother and spending her hours doing charity work to posing in front of a camera.[2]

Nothing we can build on our own is indestructible — not ships, not fame, not fortune, nor a reputation based on beauty. None of these things lasts. Power, prestige, possessions, and beauty cannot bring lasting peace or joy. As a matter of fact, they often get in the way.

But God offers us permanent and abundant peace and joy when we accept His offer of forgiveness through Jesus Christ. Once we become His children, He promises us that *nothing* can ever separate us from His love or ruin His plans for our life. One of my favorite passages in the Bible is found in Romans 8. Verse 35 asks this question:

> Who shall separate us from the love of Christ? Shall trouble or hardship or persecution or famine or nakedness or danger or sword?

Verses 38 and 39 reply:

> For I am convinced that neither death nor life, neither angels nor demons, neither the present nor the future, nor any powers, neither height nor depth (I can just picture Paul here — running out of opposite extremes, spreading his arms, shaking his head, and proclaiming in his strong Jewish accent), nor anything else in all creation, will be able to separate us from the love of God that is in Christ Jesus our Lord.

Wow! Talk about security! Once we become God's children, *nothing* can ever separate us from His love! That means that when the time comes for us to leave this planet, we will continue to live with Him forever in the wonder and excitement of heaven. If we could just grasp this concept, no one else's opinion of who we are or how God made us could ever cause us to feel insecure again.

The bottom line is this: God loves us — and nothing can change that fact! He doesn't measure His love according to the grades we received on our geometry tests; or the status of the people we eat lunch with in the school cafeteria; or the reflections of our bodies in store windows at the mall. God loves us completely just the way we are because *we are His children!*

SUMMARY

God has offered each of us an awesome identity. When we accept His gift of forgiveness through Jesus' death on the cross, we become His children. That means we are sons and daughters of the King of the universe! All the power and prestige of His kingdom are available to us.

God has given us tremendous dignity. He loved each of us so much that He was willing to sacrifice His own Son so that He could call us His children. We are worth as much to Him as the most valuable treasure He owned. And He intricately designed each of us with a specific plan and purpose. God also promises us indestructible security. Nothing and no one can ever separate us from His love.

In a world that often feels hostile and harsh, we can successfully and joyfully accomplish all that God has planned for us if we understand who we really are, what we are really worth, and where we are ultimately headed.

ISSUE #2

Why Am I Here?

As soon as you learned to throw a baseball and handle a fielder's mitt, we signed each of you up to play T-ball, an elementary version of baseball. Every inning was filled with learning experiences and funny surprises. You guys couldn't wait to put on your uniforms and head to the ball field — and we couldn't wait to watch.

During one game, while it was Matthew's turn to stand on the pitcher's mound, a little girl came up to bat for the other team. She swung as hard as she could and barely hit the ball off the tee. It dribbled slowly down the third baseline. MattE, I remember watching you dart off the mound and scoop it up before it could reach the immobile third baseman. Because you didn't trust either your own throwing accuracy or your first baseman's catching ability, you held onto the ball and chased after the little girl. By the time you got close to her, she had rounded the bag at first and was heading for second.

The parents from her team were going crazy. "Go back! Go back to first base!" they yelled, realizing that you could easily run her down and tag her out. But oblivious to their directions, she continued chugging toward second.

Meanwhile our team's parents were screaming at you, "Tag her! Tag her!" But instead of trying to reach her, you decreased your pace and jogged along behind her, maintaining a distance of about two feet. Despite the noise of the crowd I could hear you urging her on, "Run, little girl. Run!"

"Stop!" you ordered her as soon as she got to second. "Stay there and you'll be safe." Then you ran back to the mound and held up the ball to signal the end of the play.

"What was that all about?" The parents looked to me in bewilderment. "Why didn't MattE tag her out?"

I didn't have a clue, so I just shrugged my shoulders — but I made it a point to ask you as soon as the game was over.

"That little girl never got past first base before," you explained to me. "I figured she would never *ever* get to second 'less I let her, and I wanted her to have the fun of it." You were smiling from ear to ear at your generous accomplishment. I gave you a high five.

Your baseball endeavors eventually led you into a world of much more intense competition. But, MattE, in that one dynamic moment, you seemed to understand the joy that comes from making someone else successful.

JESUS CAME TO SERVE

In the last chapter we looked at the events that took place on that dreadful night before Jesus was crucified. While His disciples sat around a banquet table with filthy feet disputing which one of them was the greatest, Jesus took off His outer garments, set aside all His dignity, and knelt down to wash their feet. It was the lowliest job that a servant could perform, with absolutely no promise or prestige, yet Jesus performed it with love. As a matter of fact, John 13:1 describes Jesus' actions as a demonstration of the "full extent of his love."

You see, Jesus not only knew *who He was, what He was worth,* and *where He was going, but* he also knew *why He was here*. He was here to serve. And being a servant is all about making those around us successful.

Philippians 2:6-8 tells us that although He had the very nature of God, "[Jesus] did not consider equality with God something to be grasped, but made himself nothing, taking the very nature of a *servant,* being made in human likeness. And being found in appearance as a man, he humbled himself and became obedient to death — even death on a cross!" (emphasis added).

Over and over Jesus taught His disciples that to be great in God's eyes (which is the only place it really matters) they had to abandon the world's values. Instead of promoting themselves, their new life mission was to provide for the needs of others. In order to be "first" in God's opinion, they had to accept being "last" according to the world's standards (see Mark 9:35). To be considered the "greatest," they had to become the "least" (see Luke 22:26). Jesus redefined what was important, judging it in terms of sacrifice and servanthood rather than power and prestige.

WE ARE DESIGNED TO SERVE

God created us, He loves us, and He knows what's best for our lives. And He designed us to enjoy life most, and function best, when we are *serving*. Isaiah 58:11 is a wonderful verse:

> The LORD will guide you always; he will satisfy your needs in a sun-scorched land and will strengthen your frame. You will be like a well-watered garden, like a spring whose waters never fail.

What a fantastic picture! God promises that even when everyone else around us is fainting and famished and looking like a shriveled pot of petunias, He will make us strong and healthy. Even when things are tremendously tough and relationships are really rough, we will be like a well-watered garden that is constantly replenished.

But if you turn to this passage in your Bible and look at the verses preceding this one, you will see that this fabulous promise has some conditions attached. God will fill and satisfy us *if* we provide shelter for the poor wanderer and clothing for the naked. He will give us strength *if* we do not turn away from those who are in need. He will guide us *if* we use our energy on behalf of the hungry and spend our time meeting the needs of the oppressed.

God promises that if we serve others "[our] light will rise in the darkness, and [our] night will become like the noonday" (verse 10). And then He adds the words of verse 11 that I just quoted, pledging to fulfill our needs and bring us satisfaction. Power and peace and fulfillment and joy are always dependent on service. But if we choose to stay in the dry land of selfishness, we will shrivel and die.

The world we live in, however, does not equate service with success. It treasures things like powerful positions and popularity and personal possessions and beauty, and it places them as goals on high pedestals. We are urged to spend our lives reaching for them regardless of how many people we have to step on or over as we climb to the top.

Unfortunately, when we do achieve the goals the world has set, we often find ourselves precariously perched on the top of a wall feeling a whole lot like Humpty Dumpty. We look around in dismay and ask ourselves, *"Is that all there is up here?"* Suddenly we realize that the world's idea of success is not very satisfying or secure.

Worst of all, we discover that there is seldom an easy way down without crashing to the ground. And, as Humpty Dumpty found out, after a tumble it's pretty hard to put things back together again.

Kurt Cobain, the lead singer of Nirvana — the grunge band that redefined the music of the 1990s and continues to have a large following today — found himself trapped on top of the popularity wall the world had built for him. And he couldn't get down. He had all the prestige and money and possessions and good looks that our society values. But none of them could satisfy him or give him the peace he was searching for. They only added to the pain that had begun when he was eight years old and his father left home. In complete despair he put a shotgun under his chin and pulled the trigger during the height of his popularity.

Just like Kurt, when we buy into the world's standards we often find ourselves yearning for something different, something better, something more satisfying than what we are experiencing. That's because God created us to reach for something completely different and so much better than what the world directs us toward! God wants us to serve others instead of ourselves. When we do, He promises to take care of all our needs and comfort us through all our pain.

Look again at Jesus' example. That horrible night before His death, He served in the most humble, loving way possible. He washed His disciples' feet. And do you know why He did it? John 13, verses 12-15 tell us:

> When he had finished washing their feet, he put on his clothes and returned to his place. "Do you understand what I have done for you?" he asked them. "You call me 'Teacher' and 'Lord,' and rightly

> so, for that is what I am. Now that I, your Lord and Teacher, have washed your feet, you also should wash one another's feet. I have set you an example that you should do as I have done for you."

Jesus washed the disciples' feet in order to give them (and us) an example of how to find the power and peace and fulfillment and joy that they were searching for in life. He taught us that we are to be servants — no matter what the surrounding circumstances may be.

Mother Teresa's early life paralleled that of Kurt Cobain. She, too, lost her father at a young age. He died suddenly when she was nine years old. But even in the poverty and struggles that followed, her mother was able to instill in her the importance of serving others — and what a difference that made! Together they took care of the daily needs of a dying widow, and when that sick neighbor passed away, they accepted her six children into their already destitute family.[1]

By the time Agnes Bojaxhiu (who later chose the name Teresa) was eighteen, she realized that the only times she felt true joy in her heart were when she was helping the needy. With this inner joy as her guiding compass, she began training in India, eventually working among the poorest of the poor in Calcutta. She never had a decent education, never accumulated any possessions, and never sought after any prestigious positions. Yet she caught the eye of presidents, walked beside popes, spoke before world congresses, and won the Nobel peace prize — all because she had learned the value of being a servant.

HOW CAN WE SERVE?

In my book *Sticking Up for What Is Right* I discussed the fact that as soon as we accept Jesus Christ's death on the cross as the payment for our sin, the Holy Spirit comes to live inside us. That means that the power of the Holy Spirit that raised Jesus Christ from the grave is available in our lives! (see Ephesians 1:17-20). How awesome is that! Can you imagine what He can accomplish through us if we will let Him? But God designed it so that the Holy Spirit's power is only unleashed when we are willing to serve.

Is it any wonder we often feel so unfulfilled? Here we are with the equivalent of a Corvette engine revving inside us. But instead of heading to the racetrack, where we can enjoy all the power we were designed to experience, we putter along the parkway trying to be the coolest minivan on the road.

Zach, when you chose to leave your regular seat in the cafeteria one day to eat lunch with a lonely new student, you had no idea what a great impact that simple action would have on the life of a guy who became one of your best friends. MattE, when you delivered Christmas toys to a young boy whose family had been devastated by disease, you added a sparkle of God-filled joy to their dreary lives. Benjamin, when you helped an elderly neighbor turn the lumpy mattress on her bed, her grateful heart found praise for God. Jonathan, when you decided to use your musical abilities to draw others to Christ, unbelievable opportunities for service opened for you. One day a whole assembly of students found themselves singing praises to a God most of them had never known they could approach.

Serving in a soup kitchen, baking cookies for a shut-in, shoveling snow for a single mom, setting up chairs at church, doing the dishes with a cheerful attitude — all these are acts of service that unleash the awesome power of our incredible God.

God wants to use us to make an eternal difference in the lives of others. He wants to take our talents and abilities and possessions, coupled with the power of the Holy Spirit, to do wonderful things we can't even begin to imagine. We will be astounded at the impact our lives will make.

Let me tell you about a girl whose life was very similar to that of Mother Teresa — except she was raised in wealth instead of poverty. Amy was born in northern Ireland in 1867. She admitted in her diary that, as she grew up, she was preoccupied with her social life. It was very important to her what others thought, so she was very careful about how she dressed and who she hung around with. But one Sunday, as she and her brothers returned home from church, they spotted an old woman carrying a huge bundle. They had no desire to help her because of the embarrassment it would cause them, but they knew they should. This is what Amy wrote about that incident:

> This meant facing all the respectable people who were, like ourselves, on their way home. It was a horrid moment. We were only two boys and a girl, and not at all exalted Christians. We hated doing it. Crimson all over (at least we felt crimson, soul and body of us) we plodded on, a wet wind blows in about us, and blowing, too, the rags of that poor old woman, till she seemed like a bundle of feathers and we unhappily mixed up with them.[1]

As hesitant as she was, that one act of service turned Amy Carmichael's life around. She realized that God wanted to do some powerful things through her, but she knew that she would have to stop seeking the approval of others in order for Him to use her. She began to understand that nothing was more important than living her life for Jesus. He had given up everything He owned when He came to earth to die for her, and He wanted her to give up everything she had for Him. As she put it, this meant that she had to become "dead to the world and its applause, to all its customs, fashions, and laws."[2]

God gave Amy Carmichael a tremendous love for people who were rejected by the rest of the world. Like Mother Teresa, she found herself in India, where for fifty-five years she educated and fed the neglected and forgotten children. She rescued hundreds of five- and six-year-old girls who were being sold to the temples for prostitution. She bought them with her own money and then raised them to understand how God had also paid a price for them — one much greater than hers — the life of His own Son.

Amy Carmichael, who became one of the most famous missionaries of all time, understood that nothing was more important than serving Jesus Christ, and nothing could be more fulfilling. God wants to do amazing things through your life, but first you must be willing to serve. He probably won't take you to India — or even to Africa. He'll probably choose to use you right where you are. Wherever it is, it will be a place of great blessing.

What is the highest hope you have as a teenager? Do you dream that one day you will live in the White House as President of the United States? Do you want your likeness reproduced in granite because of some great achievement, or would you like your name inscribed on a bronze plaque for some act of generosity? Is your best hope a bit of memorabilia in a sports hall of fame or a couple of paragraphs in an alumni directory? Don't all these things seem trite compared to real peace and joy and fulfillment — not to mention a hug from the King of kings? Wouldn't you rather receive the kind of power and prestige and honor and rewards *He* offers than those offered by the world?

SUMMARY

Jesus dedicated His life to meeting the needs of others. His servant's heart and actions were in direct opposition to the standards and values of His world, and they do not measure up to the goals and principles of our world either. But when Jesus washed the feet of His disciples, He set an example for us to follow.

The power of the Holy Spirit that lives inside all believers is unleashed when we are willing to serve. He wants to take *whatever* gifts and talents we have and use them to accomplish great things for God in the lives of others. In the process we will find the true joy, peace, and fulfillment that our world is desperately seeking.

ISSUE #3

WHAT IF THINGS FROM MY PAST *Have Messed Up My Future?*

AFTER READING THE FIRST TWO CHAPTERS, YOU MIGHT BE THINKING SOMEthing like, "All this talk about finding joy and peace by being a servant might work for other people, but it will never work for me. Too much stuff has already gone wrong in my life for God to want to use anything I can offer Him."

Well, let me try to encourage you. No matter what has taken place, your life still has tremendous potential because God has incredible power! He wants to do unbelievable things in and through you! You don't have to be trapped by your past. You only have to remain its *victim* as long as you choose to!

Let me explain. A person who is raped or molested early in life, whose life then falls into a shambles due to the fear and pain produced by that abuse, is a *victim* of his or her past. However a person who is raped or molested but allows God to use and eventually overcome the resulting fear and pain is a *survivor!* A person who makes unwise choices and then finds himself unable to function due to feelings of shame or worthlessness remains a *casualty* of those choices. However, a person who seeks forgiveness and restoration through God's power can become a *conqueror.*

Satan wants us to feel like victims. He rejoices when we become casualties, because he wants us to alienate ourselves from God's love and care. He wants us to feel incapable of becoming all that God desires for us to be.

But God has incredible plans for each one of us regardless of what has taken place earlier in our lives. Listen to what He said to the Israelites who had chosen to be involved in some of the most horrible things we can imagine: "'For I know the plans I have for you,' declares the LORD, 'plans to prosper you and not to harm you, plans to give you hope and a future'" (Jeremiah 29:11). And in Job 42:2, we are told that no plan of God's can ever be ruined by anyone else. The only person who can keep you from conquering your past and experiencing a wonderful future is *you!*

SCAR TISSUE CAN HARM AS WELL AS HEAL

Zach, I'm sure you remember the summer after your junior year in high school when you played on a baseball team in Pennsylvania. Because you were left-handed and had a nasty curve ball, you quickly made the starting rotation. Normally you pitched every third or fourth day, but when the Steel Valley Palominos made a run for the championship at the end of the season, you found yourself pitching more frequently. When your team made the final round of the play-offs, you were on the mound three games in a row! Although your arm grew tired, I guess you figured you would have plenty of time to rest it during the fall. Certainly by the time the baseball season rolled around in the spring, you'd be ready to throw again.

That fall you lifted weights and worked out every day to get ready for your senior season on the mound. You hoped to have a good enough year to earn a scholarship to a Division 1 college. But then came that day in December: you were tossing bread to some seagulls, and you felt an excruciating pain in your left elbow. After a few moments you realized that you could no longer throw a piece of bread to a bird, much less hurl a baseball across home plate!

That week you began a medical odyssey that took you through just about every kind of doctor's office imaginable. You were poked and prodded, x-rayed and MRI'd. Your arm was placed in a cast for three weeks, and twice it was shot with cortisone to relieve the pain. Nobody could figure out what was wrong, and no remedy attempted offered any hope of salvaging your senior year on the mound. Instead, your arm kept growing worse.

Finally an orthopedic surgeon informed us that you needed to give up your dream of playing baseball in college. But you were not about to let the game you loved depart so easily from your life. If you couldn't pitch, you would figure out a way to play first base — the position that required the least amount of throwing.

We scheduled an appointment with a physical therapist, hoping to get you some relief from the pain and perhaps a little more range of motion so you could at least be able to toss the ball back to the pitcher on a pick-off play. Unbelievably, ten minutes after we walked into his office he had diagnosed the root of your problem! Even though it was your elbow that hurt, he discovered that you had torn the muscles of your forearm — probably by overusing it the previous summer. The initial tear had healed, but the scar tissue had continued to grow. Whenever you flexed your arm, the inflexible scar tissue around those muscles caused great stress on your elbow, resulting in agonizing pain. And all the previous remedies — immobilizing your arm, shots of cortisone, and so on — had actually done more harm than good.

After just a few weeks of exercise and deep massage therapy, the scar tissue was pulled away from the muscle, and your arm was able to function normally again. With continued exercise, no more scarring took place. You were able to finish your senior season with a strong, healthy arm, and you went on to play baseball at Florida State. You even had the privilege of going to the College World Series three out of the four years that you attended college!

All of us realize that physical injuries are an inevitable part of living on this planet. Zach certainly does! But did you know that emotional injuries are, too? Sometimes other people inflict them on us, and other times our own poor choices lead to embarrassment or shame. Either way, wounds result.

Unfortunately, during the healing process we sometimes allow emotional scar tissue to build up around an injury and cause further damage. This happens when we replay virtual videotapes of the painful event(s) over and over in our minds. Instead of letting the wounds heal, we pile more and more pain on top. Scar tissue in the form of resentment, bitterness, anger, or shame builds up around the initial injury that otherwise could have healed. We become immobilized and the pain gets worse. In the end, the scar tissue causes more pain than the original injury.

GOD WANTS TO REMOVE THE SCAR TISSUE FROM OUR LIVES

Joseph (whose story is found in Genesis 37) was a young boy when he first experienced great agony in his life. His ten older brothers were big bullies. They continually taunted and abused him and even sold him into slavery! Then, while diligently serving his master in a foreign land, he was falsely accused of sexually harassing his master's wife, and he was sentenced to prison. There he was forgotten. Joseph was alone and unloved by any standards the world had established. Yet Joseph did not become bitter or angry or resentful.

God finally rescued him, removed him from prison, and placed him in a position of power and authority in Egypt. And amazingly — after all he had been through — Joseph never retaliated against those who tried to harm him. I'm fairly certain that if I had been Joseph, I would have chartered the first chariot headed north and confronted those brothers who put me in a well and shipped me out of town. I know I would have found a way to make the woman who falsely accused me wish she had never met me. But let's look at what Joseph did instead.

Genesis 41:51 tells us that Joseph named his first son Manasseh "because God has made me forget all my trouble and all my father's household." This doesn't mean that God gave Joseph a sudden case of amnesia. No, Joseph didn't forget the names of his brothers or the things that they had done to him. He always remembered the wicked intentions of their hearts. But he allowed God to take away the scar tissue — the stinging hurt, the loathing disgust, the stewing anger — that could have destroyed his future.

Joseph was able to leave behind the painful experiences and allow God to help him go on with his life. As a matter of fact, he named his second son Ephraim "because God has made me fruitful in the land of my suffering" (verse 52). Yes, Joseph's past was filled with a lot of painful baggage, but he didn't let it ruin his future. He let God take him to magnificent places. He eventually became one of the most powerful men in the world, and God used him to save thousands of people from starvation.

You will never be able to completely forget all the painful things that take place in your life — nor should you. But as you look back at them, you should begin to see God's power and provision and direction in your life. And you should begin to experience His healing power.

After he rose to prominence Joseph was reunited with his brothers. That could have been a hurtful, hateful encounter, but instead, it became a time of healing. Joseph was eventually able to look his brothers straight in the eyes and say, "You intended to harm me, but God intended it for good to accomplish what is now being done, the saving of many lives" (Genesis 50:20).

God can break through the scar tissue in your life and set you free, too. But you have to let Him. You have to go to Him and ask Him to help you — right where you are, right now!

In his book *Please Don't Tell My Parents*, Dawson McAllister tells the story of an incredible teenager he calls JoAnn. Early in her life her mother's boyfriend abused her sexually, and the state placed her in a foster group home. She was separated from her mother and both her brothers. To make matters worse, JoAnn had scoliosis, which caused a hump to grow in her back. A surgically inserted rod caused the curve to "chill out" a little (in her own words), but her back remained crooked. She wrote a letter to Dawson explaining the incredible amount of razzing she took every day from the kids at school. They actually punched her, laughed at her, and talked down to her as if she were mentally retarded. But this was her response to the situation: "The most exciting thing about all this that is going on is God must be planning one heck of a ministry for me. He has already given me an excellent testimony."[1]

Wow! I can't even begin to imagine the fabulous things that that young lady has already accomplished for God. There were fresh wounds in her life just about every day, yet she didn't allow scar tissue to form. She understood her incredible worth to God — her real Father.

GOD WANTS TO DEMONSTRATE HIS HEALING POWER

Day after day a ragged man sat outside the temple in Jerusalem begging for food. He had done nothing to deserve his status as an outcast — except to be born blind. Based on a congenital imperfection, he was discarded by society. The Pharisees proclaimed that he was unclean and unwanted. He was not allowed to worship or walk or eat or talk with those who were "righteous" and "whole." And he certainly was not permitted to enter their sacred temple to worship their holy God!

When Jesus' disciples unkindly pointed out the beleaguered beggar, Jesus had compassion on him and cured him, performing a miracle that could only have been accomplished by the Son of God. According to John 9:6-7, Jesus spat on the ground and made some mud. Then He placed the mud on the blind man's eyes and sent him to the pool of Siloam to wash. I'm not sure what choice he really had — since Jesus had just stuck mud in his face! — but he obeyed, and when he returned he could see.

Yet, even with his sight restored, the leaders of the community continued to reject him. Once again he was forbidden to enter the temple to worship. Jesus, hearing of society's continued abuse, looked for the man. The Bible doesn't tell us where Jesus found him, but it *does* tell us how long He searched — until He found him. It was probably on the other side of the railroad tracks (make that "the donkey trail") in the middle of some stinking slum, but there Jesus chose to reveal His true identity to that unwanted man. That day, a helpless, hopeless human, who was powerless on his own to discard his past, met and worshiped God outside of the temple in a way that none of those self-righteous Pharisees would ever meet or worship Him on the inside. I don't think the beggar, who had once been blind, ever again regretted his past. It led him to a glorious present and a much-anticipated future. God used the situation to bring glory to Himself and great joy to that man.

GOD RUNS TO MEET US WHEN WE TURN TO HIM FOR HELP

God loves every one of us whose past has been torn and tattered. It doesn't matter whether the injuries came from the hurtful hands of others or if they were caused by our own unwise choices and foolish mistakes. I'm sure you know the parable Jesus told in Luke 15. It's called *The Parable of the Prodigal Son*, but I think it should be called *The Parable of the Loving Father*. In this story, a wayward, self-centered son (who represents some of us) messes up his life so miserably that the only way he can survive is to head back home, admit how wrong he has been, and beg for his father's mercy.

Meanwhile, the father (who represents God) has been watching and waiting and hoping for his child to return. When one day he sees the young man coming down the path, he does an amazing thing — he *runs* to meet him! This was a tremendously undignified reaction for a grown man in that society, but nonetheless the father hikes up his robe and runs! With his turban toppling and his sandals flip-flopping, he sprints to meet his ungrateful son.

Did you get that? God *runs* to meet us the second we turn to Him and ask for help! He can't wait to help us fix our lives and ditch our dreadful past. He doesn't force Himself on us, but He loves us so much that He doesn't want to waste one second of the time we are willing to spend with Him. The story goes on to say that the father fully restored all the rights that his son had rebelliously given up. Never did the son's past unwise choices and foolish mistakes get in the way of his restoration.

GOD SEARCHES FOR US WHEN WE ARE TOO ASHAMED TO APPROACH HIM ON OUR OWN

Adam, the first man ever created, messed up his life (and ours) in a BIG way! When he realized the horrific consequences of his dreadful decision to disobey God, he was so ashamed that he hid from God. He was devastated, humiliated, and unable to resolve the situation. If ever anyone needed a mulligan in life, it was Adam — but there were no "do-overs" available.

Adam's choices must have broken God's heart, yet how did He respond? He didn't despise Adam or want to dispose of him. He wanted to be with him. He wanted to restore the friendship and fellowship that they had previously enjoyed. He wanted to begin a healing process that would guarantee a wonderful future for Adam and all of his children for all generations. God searched for Adam. He called out to him. He wasn't satisfied until he found him (see Genesis 3:8-9).

When we are in the middle of our darkest moments, if we will just lift up our eyes we will see God coming to meet us. If we will open our ears we will hear Him calling our name. Oh, it won't be visible or audible, but it will be unmistakable!

GOD CAN USE PEOPLE NO MATTER HOW DAMAGED THEIR PASTS MAY BE

God took Rahab, a prostitute who wanted to clean up her life, and He placed her in the ancestral line of Jesus Christ. He took a murderer named Saul, changed his name to Paul, and sent him to preach the gospel to the ends of the earth. He took a man who was possessed by demons, set him free from his bondage, and sent him off as a missionary to the cities east of the Jordan River. God's inventory of "lousy lives made wonderfully whole" includes liars and lunatics and loners and losers. He makes a practice of loving the unloved and making holy the unholy and touching the untouchable and repairing them all to do wonderful things!

While Jesus was here on earth, He had a reputation for fixing broken people. He didn't waste much time on the nice, neat, "all-together" folks in His world. He restored those who knew they couldn't restore themselves. And sometimes those people wound up turning the world upside down (see Acts 17:6).

WE MUST BE WILLING TO LET GO OF THE PAST AND LET GOD HANDLE THE FUTURE

Before he met Christ on the road to Damascus, Paul caused a lot of pain in the lives of the believers — pain that could have filled his future with shame and remorse. But God had plans for his life, and Paul had to move beyond his past in order to fulfill them. In Philippians 3:13-14, he summarized his life's philosophy at that point by saying, "Forgetting what is behind and straining toward what is ahead, I press on toward the goal to win the prize for which God has called me heavenward in Christ Jesus." This does not mean that he pretended that all the things he had ever done never took place, or deluded himself into believing that all the pompous things he had built himself up to be never existed. The Greek word that is translated *forgetting* means that he "stopped recalling information" concerning what had taken place. With God's help he stopped replaying the old videotapes in his head and was able to recognize the brand-new future that God was offering him.

We, too, with God's help, must stop regretting what has taken place in our pasts. That is what Joseph did, and that is what Paul tells us to do. That means we must be willing to drop any resentment or bitterness or anger or shame that have built up like scar tissue around the places where we hurt. It doesn't matter if others inflicted the wounds or we caused them ourselves.

We must refuse to watch shadowy reruns of old videos that recall past hurts. Instead we must fill our minds with the beautiful stories God has recorded for us in the Bible — stories of the healing He has performed in the lives of others. He can do the same life-changing things for us. He has already written wonderful scripts, and He is anxious to direct and produce brand-new videos of our lives.

And we must be willing to move on. We must allow God to handle any restoration and let *Him* take care of any retaliation that is necessary. His specialty is making wrong things right. He wants to remove the past pain and make our lives peaceful and playful again.

Sometimes we will find this process too difficult or painful to accomplish on our own. That is why God has positioned parents and youth pastors and church leaders in our lives. They are supposed to give us guidance and support when we need it most. Christian counselors are trained for this very purpose. God will always provide us with help when we need it. But we must be willing to accept it.

Jeremiah 32:17 is one of my favorite verses. "Ah, Sovereign LORD, you have made the heavens and the earth (and *me*) by your great power and outstretched arm. *Nothing* is too hard for you" (insert and emphasis added). Don't ever sell God short. Don't ever think that too much has already gone wrong in your life for Him to be able to fix and use you. After all, we're talking about a God who was able to make a blind man see — using nothing more than mud and spit! Just think what He can do for you if you will let Him!

SUMMARY

Events from our past don't have to ruin our future. God has wonderful plans for each one of us. Each of us has suffered injuries —

wounds that have been inflicted by our own unwise decisions or by the damaging actions of others. But we must not allow the "scar tissue" of resentment or bitterness or anger or shame to build up around those injuries and make them even worse.

God wants to remove the scar tissue. He wants to demonstrate His healing power in our lives. He will run to meet us the second we turn to Him for help, and He will search for us when we are too ashamed to approach Him on our own. He wants to repair and restore and use us to accomplish wonderful things.

ISSUE #4

What If Others Make *Fun of My Faith?*

Long before any of you were born I worked as a nurse in a small hospital. It was a part-time job until my real job as a school nurse started in the fall. While I was there I met a young lady who was recuperating from a complicated back surgery. I felt sorry for her because she had to lie flat on her bed twenty-four hours a day, so I often visited her during my breaks. I asked if I could pray for her one day when she was struggling through a lot of pain, and I learned that she, too, was a believer. She and her husband, David, had asked Jesus Christ into their lives at a Billy Graham crusade just a few months before.

During those long summer weeks that Candy was hospitalized we were able to share many conversations about our mutual faith. Sometimes I would sit and read stories to her from the Bible. By the time she left the hospital we were great friends.

As Candy recuperated, she and David and Dad and I began to spend a lot of time together. We went camping and sailing and enjoyed long evenings chatting out under the stars on the balcony of their apartment. No matter what we did, the conversation always centered on God and the plans that He had for our lives. Dad had just started his seminary training, so he often shared the things he learned in his classes. Candy and David couldn't seem to grow fast enough in their newfound faith. They were always eager to learn more, and their enthusiasm was contagious.

Soon Candy was well enough to return to her job as a flight attendant. The time we were able to spend together decreased, but we always stayed in touch. When they moved into a new home a few weeks before Christmas, Candy and David decided to celebrate by inviting all their new neighbors in for a big party. They couldn't wait to share with everyone all that God was doing in their lives and why Christmas was so special to them.

We were out of town and unable to attend, but Candy was a fabulous entertainer, so I'm sure that the house was beautiful and the food was great. They told us later that all the guests were having a wonderful time, and the new home was filled with laughter and Christmas music and fun — until David gathered everyone together in the living room and opened his Bible. He read the story of the birth of Christ and explained how his guests could experience the joy of that very first Christmas morning.

The party instantly dropped dead! People politely thanked David and Candy for opening their home, but they seemed to want to get out of there as quickly as possible. Within a few minutes the house was silent, except for the Christmas carols playing in the family room.

David and Candy were devastated. Instead of attracting others to their new faith, their enthusiasm had scared people away. They felt alienated from their neighbors and ostracized from neighborhood functions. People would politely nod or wave when they walked past the house, but no one cared to stop and talk or develop any kind of relationship with them. It seemed that their disastrous party had become the gossip of the neighborhood.

How could the very thing that brought them the most joy in life suddenly bring them so much pain? The ridicule was almost more than they could bear.

But they did not give up. Slowly, over the next year as neighbors became ill or faced tragedies, David and Candy stepped in to meet needs and provide companionship. One by one, they formed meaningful friendships and relationships. Over the course of several years, God used the party that had caused David and Candy great pain to heal many much-deeper wounds.

YOU CAN EXPECT RIDICULE AS A REACTION TO YOUR FAITH

It is difficult to find examples of men or women of faith in the Bible who were *not* ridiculed or reviled in some way for their convictions. Noah was laughed at for 120 years when he decided to obey God. Everyone pointed their fingers and scoffed at him when he started to build a huge boat in the middle of his backyard. How was he going to get that thing to the ocean? There was no water anywhere in sight — not a single river nearby to float it down. When he tried to explain his actions and warn his neighbors that God was planning to destroy the earth with a great flood, the laughter grew even louder. He became the object of every child's snicker and the punch line for every comedian's joke — until the rain started!

And Moses! He had just finished performing monumental miracles through the power of God. It was because of Moses' faith that the Israelites had been set free from their torturous bondage in Egypt, and it was because of his leadership that they had been able to walk across the Red Sea on dry land. But they had hardly finished singing the wonderful song of praise recorded in Exodus 15:1-21 when they started to gripe and complain. *Just three verses later*, instead of honoring Moses, they are dumping all over him. As soon as they got hungry and thirsty they began to ridicule his leadership and faith. "What are we to drink?" they mockingly questioned him when they came to a spring in Marah that spouted only bitter water (see verse 24). He was taunted by the very people he had just helped. In just a few miles Moses went from a hero to a zero in their eyes.

You've heard of Hannah, haven't you? The people she lived with belittled her because she couldn't have any children. She was ridiculed for her faith in a God who had obviously, according to their cultural priorities, abandoned her. When she fervently prayed that He would open her womb and send her a son, the priest scolded her for acting like she was drunk. But because of her faith, God eventually blessed her. She gave birth to Samuel, who became the most famous judge to rule the nation of Israel.

And what about Paul? He was constantly run out of towns and tormented for his faith. When he finally got a chance to participate in the Super Bowl of all philosophical events that took place in Athens on Mars Hill, he bombed. It was an opportunity he had eagerly anticipated as a chance to influence the most intellectual people in the world with the facts of Christianity, but he was basically laughed off the stage. Acts 17:32 tells us that the men who ran the event actually "sneered" at his words and forced him out of their presence. Only a few men and a couple of women stuck around to listen to what he had to say. But that treatment was minor compared to what Paul normally endured as he stood up for his faith. In 2 Corinthians 11:23-28 he tells us about the frequent floggings, imprisonments, cold, hunger, and stoning he survived.

The treatment Paul constantly faced after he accepted Jesus as his Savior was far worse than anything you or I will ever experience! Who do we think we are not to expect and accept a little ridicule? Why should our friends understand our priorities and lifestyle choices any better than the people in Paul's, or Hannah's, or Moses', or Noah's, or Candy's and David's lives understood theirs? Second Timothy 3:12 states it quite frankly: "In fact, everyone who wants to live a godly life in Christ Jesus will be persecuted." This is definitely not one of my favorite verses!

Some of your friends (and even some family members) will not understand that your faith requires obedience to the principles in God's Word. They may not appreciate that you refuse to attend certain events or choose to participate in activities they don't consider fun. They may not comprehend why you insist on being honest and want to stay away from things that are impure. Their lack of understanding may lead them to ridicule your choices and make fun of your actions. It's a human tendency to scoff at the things we can't explain and to belittle and try to bully those whose actions cause ours to come into question.

But ridicule does not have to result in discouragement or defeat. Instead it can cause your faith to deepen and your relationship with God to grow stronger.

YOU CAN RELY ON GOD TO GET YOU THROUGH THE RIDICULE

Several times in his role as Israel's leader, Moses was tempted to quit — to pick up his staff and go home — because of the ridicule he faced. But fortunately he never did. Instead of taking the scoffing personally, he took it to God. He allowed the derision and discouragement of others to draw him closer to his Father, rather than pull him away. He chose to value his friendship with God more than his relationships with the men and women of Israel.

Do you remember Marah, the place we just talked about that had only bitter water? There, at that spring, Moses encountered one of the many difficult tests he would face as the leader of the new nation. But instead of sulking in self-pity as the people grumbled and mocked him, Moses cried out to God for a solution. God showed Moses a piece of wood and told him to throw it into the spring. Sure enough, pure, sweet water began to bubble from the earth.

And then God did even more for Moses. He took him and his griping, complaining companions to a place called Elim where they found twelve wells of water and seventy palm trees. From a place of ridicule, bitterness, and discouragement, God took them to a place of fullness and refreshment. How did Moses get there? He simply didn't quit. He endured the ridicule and kept following and trusting God. If you look at a map of the Bible you will see that Marah and Elim are only a few miles apart — five to be exact. What a shame it would have been if Moses had given up by giving in to the mockery at Marah! He never would have experienced that beautiful resting place that God had prepared for him.

Don't let the ridicule of friends or the criticism of family members or the bullying of bystanders make you miss out on the sweet places God has planned for your journey. Don't ever let go of God in order to hold on to your friends. Instead, let go of your friends and hold on to God. Let Him take you to places of rest and restoration.

YOU CAN VIEW THE RIDICULE AS A PRECURSOR TO A REWARD

When you accept Jesus Christ as your Savior, the Holy Spirit comes to live inside of you. His power and personality are hard to contain inside a human container, and the evidence of His presence becomes obvious as you grow in your faith. It is like a light that begins to glow inside of you, and soon it is shining right through you. People cannot help but be attracted to it. But unfortunately, light not only attracts those who are seeking warmth and companionship, it also attracts *bugs*, and they can be a pain!

First Peter 4:14 says, "If you are insulted because of the name of Christ, you are blessed, for the Spirit of glory and of God rests on you." You see, the ridicule and snubbing you receive as a result of your faith in God and your obedience to Him are evidences that the glory of His Holy Spirit is shining through you.

But if you reread 2 Timothy 3:12 carefully you will see that there is a way to avoid the ridicule that we have been talking about. You could choose to live a less than godly life. Then you would never experience a snicker or a snort from friends belittling your beliefs. But, of course, you also would have to abandon the peace and joy that Jesus promises to those who put their faith into practice. You could go "underground" with your beliefs and hope that no one will ever recognize you as a child of God. That would be like covering the Holy Spirit's glow with a blanket so that no one could see it shine. But then you would miss out on all the blessings God has promised for you while you are here on earth and all the rewards that He has waiting for you in heaven. In Matthew 5:11-12, Jesus says, "Blessed are you when people insult you, persecute you and falsely say all kinds of evil against you because of me. Rejoice and be glad, because great is your reward in heaven."

Zach and Matthew, do you remember how when you first started to play high school baseball, your coach encouraged you to get up early in the morning before school to lift weights? He also expected you to stay after school to practice drills. He convinced you to go to bed early (even on weekends!) so that you could stay healthy and strong both physically and mentally. He knew that his demands were contrary to the routines accepted by the normal teenage culture, and he was wise enough to anticipate that you would take a lot of grief for such a change in your lifestyle. So he warned you that many of your friends (and maybe even your parents) would think that you were nuts. But he promised that in the long run, the hard work and the ridicule that followed would be worth it.

All through your high school years you did exactly what the coach suggested (or should that word be *demanded?*). You left the house by 5:30 A.M. to lift weights at the YMCA. You stayed long hours after school to hit in the batting cages and "long toss." You missed many events and left more than a few parties early so that you could get enough sleep to keep up with your studies and your routine.

Many of your friends scoffed at your schedule just as the coach had predicted. But you didn't mind. You trusted him that the rewards you would receive would make it all worthwhile. And they did! Winning the state championship was better than anything you could have imagined!

But that experience was nothing compared to what God has waiting for you in heaven if you are willing to accept a little ridicule for your lifestyle here on earth. First Corinthians 2:9 tells us, "No eye has seen, no ear has heard, no mind has conceived what God has prepared for those who love him."

We never dreamed that we would get to ski in Vail, Colorado — let alone spend a Christmas vacation there. It was a trip far too extravagant for us to plan. But when airline tickets and six free nights in a condominium were offered to us, we jumped at the possibility. That vacation surpassed anything we ever dreamed of! None of us will ever forget it.

We stayed in a seven-bedroom condo that was right on the slopes! Every morning right after breakfast, we would slip on our skis and head down the mountain to the lifts. When we became tired or hungry or cold, we would ski right back to the front door and head inside. We spent our evenings playing games by the fireplace or relaxing outside in the gigantic Jacuzzi. A Christmas tree lit up the whole deck, and we could sit in the warm, bubbling water catching snowflakes in our mouths and listening to Christmas carols while we looked at the sparkling lights of the village below.

Less than five minutes after we arrived we had forgotten all the trauma and toil that went into making the trip a success. Any hardships or inconveniences we endured quickly became insignificant compared to the pleasures that our destination had to offer. The delayed flights, the long lines, the lost luggage, the scary turbulence, and the long, slippery drive up the mountain in the middle of a blizzard quickly left our minds. All the things that made us question our decision to take the trip and consider turning around and heading home became trivial compared to the outcome. Vail at Christmastime was more wonderful than anything we could have ever imagined! Our only regret was that we had round-trip tickets. We eventually had to return to the "real" world of Lakeland, Florida.

Well, guess what! As fabulous as that vacation in Vail was, you have been offered an all-expense-paid trip to a place even more fantastic! When you accepted Jesus Christ as your Savior you were given a one-way ticket (that means you never have to leave!) and free lodging in the palace and playground of the King of kings!

The Bible promises us that heaven is going to be far more magnificent than anything we have ever experienced here on earth. All the beauty and relaxation and fun and pleasure that Vail has to offer are nothing compared to what we will enjoy when we arrive in heaven. However, the Bible does not promise us that the journey will be an easy one. As a matter of fact, it promises quite the opposite. In John 16:33, Jesus says, "In this world you will have trouble. But take heart! I have overcome the world."

Wouldn't it be wonderful if, when we accepted Jesus Christ as our Savior, we were immediately zapped straight to heaven for the rest of eternity? Wouldn't it be nice not to have to put up with any of the pain or suffering or teasing or torment that inevitably seem to accompany our faith? But think about it. If that happened, who would tell our friends and neighbors about Jesus Christ and how He died for them so that they, too, can enjoy the magnificence of heaven? Who would be left here on earth to provide eternal comfort and compassion for the helpless and homeless in our society? Who would be able to offer a real source of hope when devastating tragedies occur? Who would be on their knees praying for the leadership of our nation and pleading for their devotion to God's standards and principles?

God has left us here for a purpose. We have definite tasks and responsibilities that He wants us to fulfill before we can enjoy the pleasures of paradise that He has created for us. We are commissioned by God to tell everyone we meet on our journey through life how they, too, can live in heaven for all of eternity (see Matthew 28:19-20). The route we have to take will sometimes be difficult. At times it might even be treacherous. But believe me, when we stand in heaven next to those whose lives we've touched, we will gladly admit that our final destination is worth any hardship we had to endure!

SUMMARY

We cannot expect our friends who do not share the same relationship we have with God to understand our priorities and lifestyle choices any better than people understood Noah's or Moses' or Hannah's or Paul's. Ridicule is a natural reaction to things people don't understand. But ridicule does not have to result in discouragement or defeat. Instead it can cause our faith to deepen and our relationship with God to grow stronger.

God will always take us through the criticism to places of rest and refreshment—just like He did for Moses—if we allow Him to. And God has promised not only to rescue and restore us, but also to bless us if we are persecuted for His sake (see Matthew 5:11-12). The reward of an all-expense-paid, one-way trip to heaven to live with Him for eternity should cause the trials we face along the journey to seem trivial. God has left us here on earth for a reason: we are to tell others how they, too, can live with Him in all the glory of heaven for all of eternity! (see Matthew 28:19-20).

ISSUE #5

If I Had What They Have, *I'd Be Happy Too!*

There were plenty of places for first-graders to hang out at the boarding school I attended in Africa. There was a playground with swing sets and slides and monkey bars and sandboxes, and there was even a huge rock that we were allowed to climb. But none of these appealed to me. Every afternoon I became bored with my age-appropriate companions and their silly little games. Lured by the tantalizing laughter and squeals of joy that came from the "big kids," I would edge myself closer and closer to their territory. From under the shade of a mango tree I would watch for hours as they played games like stealing sticks, blindman's bluff, or red rover. I longed for the day that I would be old enough to join in.

That day came sooner than I had anticipated. One afternoon as I sat under the mango tree, the "big kids" decided to play a game of hide-and-seek. However they couldn't agree on who should be "it." They tried various methods of selecting the first player who would have to search while everyone else hid, but every time they came up with someone, that person convincingly argued his way out of the role.

Then one of the "big kids" spotted me under the mango tree. Suddenly I was thrust in the middle of the crowd and informed that not only was I allowed to play with the "big kids," but I was going to be the star of the game. They were going to let me be "it"!

I was elated. Quickly they recited the rules. They drew a huge square in the sand and informed me that this was the jail. I had to close my eyes and count to one hundred while everyone hid. Then every time I found someone, that person had to go jail. The object was for me to imprison all the upperclassmen. The first person I had captured would become the new "it," and we would play again.

The rules sounded fair enough. Dutifully I closed my eyes and counted to one hundred — as best I could. Then I hollered, "Ready or not, here I come" just like the "big kids" always did, and I began my "seeking" duties.

It didn't take long for me to find Susie Taylor. She was rather large, and I don't think she realized that the tree she was hiding behind was no match for her frame. I shouted her name and told her to go to jail.

"Uh, uh," she hollered back. "You gotta *catch* me — not just *see* me!" I didn't recall the rules being stated that way, but I took off after her. As soon as I chased her down, I escorted her to the sandy play area and deposited her in jail.

Then I took off after Tommy Barber who was taunting me from behind some flower bushes. He was fast, but he made the mistake of running around a big pile of rocks. I scrambled over the top and jumped on him. (I think he was impressed.) And off he went to jail. I was doing great and was exhilarated by the joy of participating with the "big kids."

By the time I ran down the third person, I was exhausted—and shocked to find that no one was in jail when we got there. Susie and Tommy had taken off.

"Hey, get back here. No one is allowed to escape!" I protested as I watched them disappear around the building.

"Yeah, they are," my latest detainee informed me. "Someone snuck in and freed them. It's all part of the game."

For what seemed like hours I ran and chased and captured and escorted "big kids" to jail. Every time I imprisoned two or three people, someone else would set them free. Great laughter and squeals of joy accompanied our game—but not from me! I had never been so relieved to hear the dinner bell that signaled the end of afternoon play.

The next afternoon I returned to the first-grade side of the playground and joined my classmates in a rip-roaring game of follow the leader. I didn't go anywhere near the mango tree!

My lack of contentment led me to a place where I didn't belong. Once I arrived, I realized that the new situation and set of friends did not satisfy the longings that had lured me there. Over the years God has used many such instances in my life to teach me that I must accept the circumstances He has chosen for me if I want to experience real peace and joy.

LACK OF CONTENTMENT ROBS US OF GOD'S BEST

If we took a survey, I'm sure most of your classmates would indicate that if they had a little more money, or owned a few more things, or experienced a closer relationship with a certain person, their lives would be happier and they would be more content. I am equally certain that if we could wave a magic wand and improve all of these circumstances in each of their lives today, one month from now they would still respond to the survey in exactly the same way.

Our society creates and capitalizes on discontentment. The media provokes it. Our consumer-based economy thrives on it. There always seems to be someone absent or something missing from our lives that holds the key to our satisfaction. No matter how much we've accomplished or how far we've come, there seems to be one more step we need to take before we can reach the elusive destination called happiness.

I'll never forget the time all four of you insisted that you had discovered the secret of real happiness. Somehow you convinced Dad and me that a trampoline would solve all of our family's problems. I think it was the line that went something like, "If you'll buy us a trampoline, we will never, ever, ever ask for anything else for the rest of our lives," that finally persuaded us to go ahead and purchase one. So we did, and soon all four of you were bouncing on a big blue trampoline in the middle of the backyard. Of course, six weeks later you were whining and pleading for a new puppy to play with on the trampoline!

The fact is that *nothing in this world* can give us the peace or the happiness or the fulfillment that we long for — not a cool car or a classy wardrobe or the most popular friends or a prestigious position. Possessions and popularity and positions are powerful enough to lure us into their grasp, but they are powerless to give us peace. Just like drugs, they can become intoxicating and addicting. They can enslave us so that we are not free to go to the places God wants us to go, or do the things He wants us to do, or be the people He wants us to be. We end up missing out on all the blessings He intended for us to have.

Zach wasn't exactly thrilled having to drive the Honey Wagon (a beat-up, yellow station wagon) back and forth to high school every day. Most of his friends had fabulous new cars. But given the choice to work more hours after school in order to make the payments on a newer, cooler car or play baseball, he chose baseball. Consequently, he was able to earn a scholarship and travel across the nation playing for his college. He even spent a summer in Africa where he was able to tell hundreds of children about God's love while he taught them how to play the game he enjoyed so much. He could have been lured away from baseball by a shiny, new truck like many of his friends had been, but no new vehicle could have given him the fabulous experiences or the joy that resulted from his willingness to drive a ten-year-old clunker for a few years.

One of Satan's slickest tricks is to make us think we need more than what God has provided and then trap us in the process of pursuing it. Let me tell you the story of a lady who had everything — and I mean *everything!* — that anyone could possibly desire, yet she wanted more. She was married to a wonderful man, and they lived in what we would consider a paradise. Their home was designed by the best architect, built by the finest builder, and decorated with original artwork. Not only did the lady live in comfort and luxury, she never had to cook or clean or worry about what to wear! Everything she needed was hers.

But one day a guy name Lu walked into her life and suggested that in the midst of all the beauty and affluence that was in her life, she was missing one thing — and she began to long for it. She quickly reached a point of dissatisfaction where she was willing to ignore all that was right in her life, and instead of accepting God's provision, she chose to pursue what was appealing.

Because of a terrible decision she made, she lost her home and all its wonderful amenities. Life became almost unbearable. The once-pampered lady had to learn to cook and clean and even sew her own clothes. The choice she made to pursue one more thing than God had allotted for her life reverberated forever in the lives of her children. They were never able to share the peace and joy of the life she had once lived.

In case you haven't figured it out, the story I just told you is the story of Eve. Lu, of course, is Lucifer (another name for Satan). God had created the most wonderful paradise we can possibly imagine. He had filled it with fabulous wildlife (make that "*tame* life"), capped it off with the creation of a man named Adam, and then pinnacled it with the creation of a woman named Eve. There was only one thing that they didn't have, and that was access to the tree in the middle of the garden — the Tree of the Knowledge of Good and Evil.

When Lucifer pointed out the void in her life, Eve began to desire to eat from that tree so much that she talked Adam into tasting a piece of its forbidden fruit with her. Forever their lives, and the lives of all the human beings who came after them, were altered by that sin. We have struggled ever since to trust the promises of God rather than allow ourselves to be tricked by Satan and trapped by the powerful appeal of possessions.

LACK OF CONTENTMENT REFLECTS A POOR UNDERSTANDING OF GOD'S CHARACTER

God promises that He will give us everything we need to fill our lives. In Matthew 6:25-33, Jesus tells us that it is wrong to desire more than God has provided. He points out that if we seek God's kingdom and His righteousness in our lives, God will supply us with food and clothing and anything else we need. And in 1 Timothy 6:8, we are commanded to be content with the things God provides. When we fail to acknowledge that God has placed us in the right situation or provided us with the right things or surrounded us with the right people, it is obvious that we do not comprehend His sovereignty and love.

During Old Testament times, God chose to use the nation of Israel as a lighthouse to the world. Other nations were to be drawn to Him by observing how wonderfully He blessed the Israelites when they obeyed His commandments and honored Him. He called them His children and He promised to protect them and provide for all their needs.

As His children wandered in the wilderness, God lived with them in a very special, portable building called the tabernacle. To make sure His house and His nation were well taken care of, God assigned different people different jobs. The men from the tribe of Levi were the ones responsible for the upkeep and transportation of the tabernacle. They did not have to gather food or take care of the flocks or perform any of the daily duties that consumed the lives of the other men. They did not even have to fight against the enemies who tried to ambush them. They were set apart to do the work of God.

Three different families made up this Levitical tribe, and God gave each of them different tasks. The family of Gershon was designated to take care of the huge tent that made up the tabernacle. They also handled the curtains that walled it off from the community and divided it into rooms. Merari's family had to transport and set up all the frames and posts that were used to construct the tabernacle. Kohath and his clan were responsible to care for the "most holy things" (Numbers 4:4). They transported and set up the special table, the lampstand, the altars, and all the articles of the sanctuary that were used by the priests when they were ministering. And the Kohathites were the only ones allowed to carry the ark — God's holy dwelling place!

The only Israelites with more responsibility than the Kohathites were the priests (Aaron and his sons). They were allowed to enter God's holy presence and light the altars with the special fire that God had provided.

But Korah, the leader of the Kohathite family, became jealous of the priests' responsibilities. *He* wanted to enter the holiest place and ask God to forgive the sins of the people. *He* wanted to carry the special fire and light the sacrifices. His jealously led to bitterness and discontentment, and soon he devised a plot to procure the position of the priests. Numbers 16 tells the story of his rebellion. It tells how he gathered the leaders of two other families and 250 grumbling men around him and went to Moses to demand a better position.

Moses fell on his face in extreme sadness when he was confronted by Korah's dissatisfaction and in verses 7, 9-10 he replied:

> You Levites have gone too far! . . . *Isn't it enough* for you that the God of Israel has separated you from the rest of the Israelite community and brought you near himself to do the work at the LORD's tabernacle and to stand before the community and minister to them? He has brought you and all your fellow Levites near himself, but now you are trying to get the priesthood too (emphasis added).

"Isn't it enough, Korah?" Moses responded in righteous indignation. "Look at the special position God has given you, yet you aren't satisfied. He has set you apart and given you access to the most holy things that any human being could handle, and you are choosing to complain. How dare you!"

God designed a contest that would show the whole nation who should carry the holy fire and represent the Israelite people before Him. To make a long story short, Korah lost the contest. He and his two discontented companions were buried alive when the earth opened up under their feet. Holy fire came down from heaven and consumed the rest of the 250 complaining community leaders! (I can just hear God saying, "So you want to handle holy fire, huh? Well, here . . . handle this!")

Sometimes it may not seem like a lot, guys, but what God has given each one of us *IS EXACTLY ENOUGH!* He knows *exactly* what is required to handle the tasks that He has prepared for us today. He has the power to give us whatever we need — after all, He owns everything on this planet. And He loves us enough to give us what is best. How dare any of us choose to be discontent!

CONTENTMENT IS A CHOICE

Just last week I met a teenager (I'll call him Jeremy) at a youth leadership conference. It was the first day of the conference, and we were both grabbing a last-minute cup of coffee before the morning meeting began. I watched as Jeremy stirred three packets of sugar into a cup filled with one part coffee and two parts cream. With a shy, embarrassed grin he started to explain his concoction, but for some reason he stopped in the middle and inquired, "Are you having a good day?"

"I sure am," I replied. "How about you?"

His words were slow and deliberate. "I am. I really, really am." He let out a deep breath, then thoughtfully began to list all the things that God had already done for him that day. He had enjoyed a hot shower, eaten a wonderful breakfast, gone for a walk in the woods, and listened to some great music. Everything I had taken for granted seemed to evoke gratefulness in Jeremy's heart. We talked for a few minutes longer, and then each entered the meeting through a different door.

There was something wistful about Jeremy and his outlook on

life. I had to know more about him, so I made it a point to run into him several times during the next few days. He never answered my questions quickly but was always reflective, and his answers were always centered on what God had done for him. His gentle spirit and constant gratefulness fascinated me.

As the week progressed and I got to know him better, I discovered that Jeremy's father had died when he was very young. He had been raised in a home filled with alcoholism and abuse. Irate landlords had often evicted his family from run-down apartments. He had lived in shelters and seedy motels for much of his life. Yet Jeremy insisted that God had always provided for him. "God always took care of me. He always knew what I needed," he explained.

When his grandfather — the only man who had ever loved and cared for him — died a few years ago as a result of alcoholism, Jeremy adopted a counterculture outlook and a destructive attitude. But when he walked into a church one day, some of the kids from the youth group invited him to join them. They insisted on loving him despite his weird hairdo and Gothic attire. Jeremy was overwhelmed by their acceptance and friendship. It wasn't long before he embraced the love of their God and the sacrifice of Jesus Christ.

Difficulties continued to haunt Jeremy and his family. The latest of his many stepfathers had died of cancer just a month before we met, and another abusive man had already taken his place. But Jeremy knew that God would somehow use the situation to bring about good. "I know God will use everything that's going on," he insisted. "Somehow it's going to be an important part of how He wants to use me."

Judging by any standards that I know, Jeremy's upbringing was not adequate to produce gratefulness. Yet his heart overflowed with gratitude for all of God's provisions. Jeremy did not allow the terrible circumstances he found himself in to imprison him. Instead of viewing them as a source of *confinement,* he chose to see them as his *assignment.* Instead of considering his situation to be a *penalty,* he accepted it as part of God's *plan.* His contentment in the face of tremendous adversity greatly impacted my life.

Contentment does not require developing a phony attitude of gratitude for the circumstances we find ourselves in. But it does involve making a choice to trust God with what He has given us. And then we must make an effort to use what we've been given to bring Him glory. Contentment is not contingent on the people, places, or things in our lives. It is contingent on how much we choose to trust God.

SUMMARY

Satan can rob us of all that God has planned for our lives by tricking us into thinking that we need more than what God has provided and then by trapping us in the process of pursuing it. He uses the lure of better possessions or greater popularity or more productive friendships or more prestigious positions to deceive us into thinking that God does not understand our predicament, or that He does not have the power to improve our situation, or that He doesn't love us enough to give us what is best for our lives.

When we fail to acknowledge that God has placed us in exactly the right situation or provided us with exactly the right things or surrounded us with exactly the right people, it is because we do not comprehend His sovereignty or trust His wisdom. Finding contentment involves making a choice to trust God with our circumstances — and then making an effort to use what He has given us to bring Him glory.

ISSUE #6

Why Do I Feel So Angry *So Often?*

What's up with this? Your baseball team had just slaughtered the other team, and when you came out of the dugout I congratulated you. All I said was, "Good game, Ben" — and YOU BLEW UP AT ME!

"*Good!* Did you say '*Good*'?" you snarled. Then an emphatic "Paahhh!" burst out of your mouth mixed with a little spit. "Don't talk to me about '*Good!*'"

You had just crouched behind home plate for the better part of two hours on a hot, humid afternoon wearing about twenty pounds of catcher's gear, and you had done an excellent job. Very few balls had gotten past your glove. You had even made a diving catch on a foul pop-up to end one of the innings. Then you had made an outstanding play on a wild pitch to save the pitcher's stats. I could think of play after play that deserved recognition, so I tried to defend my comment — only to cause another explosion.

"You obviously didn't see my throw to third when their guy was stealing," you growled. "I should have had him by a mile! But, no! What did I do? I launched the ball clear into left field!"

I didn't know enough to shut up. "Hey, the batter got in your way. There was no way you could have gotten off a clean throw," I argued. "Besides, the guy didn't even end up scoring."

"I stunk it up, Mom! Quit trying to make me into some kind of hero!" you hollered, heaving your gear into the backseat of the car.

I was ticked. I knew that I was right. You had played a very good game and you deserved credit, and if I wanted to give it to you, you certainly should have been willing to accept it. But even more than that, I certainly didn't deserve to be hollered at. I was about to unload my hurt feelings on you, but for some reason I decided to keep my mouth shut.

We drove home in silence and, except for one statement, neither of us spoke for the next couple of hours. "I love you, Ben," I said softly as I handed you a sandwich. You didn't respond.

So, how could one simple, honest statement cause so much anger to suddenly burst out of your adolescent heart and mouth? It's a question that teenagers and their parents have been asking for generations.

WHERE DOES THIS ANGER COME FROM?

As a teenager you are dealing with incredible changes in your physical being, and the factors that cause your body to grow place tremendous demands on your feelings as well. Emotions are very powerful and run very deep during the teenage years. The sudden onslaught of puberty brings with it hormones that heighten just about every reaction. Pleasures are more stimulating; adventures are more exciting; uncertainties are more frightening; frustrations are more exasperating. For this reason, simple things that would only be viewed as an annoyance at another time in your life can trigger intense anger. Sometimes you will explode without even knowing why.

Many factors affect your ability to handle the emotions and feelings that suddenly enter your life. The amount of sleep you get greatly influences your mental capability to handle stress. Due to the nature of hormones, one minute you are bursting with energy and the next you are dead tired. This can cause you to feel out of control. Often you are unable to predict your own response to a situation. Your health also has an effect on your ability to handle your emotions. When your physical defenses are diminished, so is your emotional stamina. And your social situation (how you did on your last geography quiz or who ignored you at the last school social) has a great deal to do with your ability to handle the irritations you encounter.

Another cause of anger during your teenage years is the changing role you face in your family. You are in a rather precarious position. Although you are clamoring for more independence and freedom, you are not ready (or sometimes willing) to accept the accompanying responsibilities. You want unlimited freedom in choosing your own friendships and managing you own schedule. Yet you expect your meals to be taken care of, your doctors visits to be scheduled, the electricity that powers your computer and CD player to be paid for, and some kind of budget to be provided for your clothing.

Conflicts are inevitable as you feel the need for more independence and your parents (the poor people assigned to guide you through all this) realize your limitations in handling total freedom. What we view as "protection" you may interpret as "lack of trust," leaving you feeling frustrated and angry. Curfews are a constant source of such irritation. We recognize the necessity of sleep for your physical and emotional well-being. You feel you can function just fine without it. We have adopted the principle that "nothing good happens after midnight." You are sure that "nothing exciting happens *before* midnight." We feel that curfews are necessary for your welfare. You feel they belittle our faith in you.

Other changes in your home life can trigger anger as well. If a family is dealing with the stress of marital problems or sickness or financial pressure, teenagers may find themselves feeling overlooked or lonely. They may begin to harbor a low-grade anger just below the surface of their everyday emotions. They become like an ember that is about to burst into flame the second a gust of wind comes along.

IS IT OKAY TO EXPRESS MY ANGER?

In the midst of all the turmoil of being a teenager all it takes is one misunderstood comment, one misplaced pair of blue jeans, or one mistake on a test to set all the pieces in place for an angry flare-up. I soon found out that Ben's heated comments had nothing to do with my enthusiastic response to his ball game or my desire to be an encouraging mom. They had everything to do with the fact that he thought he had bombed a science test earlier that morning. He had been holding on to his feelings of frustration and anger all day, and he let them fly at the first safe target that he encountered — me.

Was it okay for Ben to blow up at me?

No, it wasn't! Ninety-nine percent of the time when we become angry it is because we are being selfish. Someone or something has intruded on what we consider to be our space, our time, our possessions, or our rights. In other words, we become angry because things don't go our way. If we are honest, we have to admit that most of our anger comes from feeling that we are better, smarter, or more deserving than others.

This was true in Ben's case. He was angry because he felt that the science test was very unfair. If he had taken the time to analyze his anger, he might have realized that he was upset because he felt that his rights had been violated. (Obviously he deserved a simpler test.) Or perhaps he felt that he was smarter than the teacher. (*He* could have created a test that would have been a much more accurate assessment of his knowledge.) In either case, his anger was motivated by selfishness.

But once Ben became angry, wasn't it much better for him to get the anger out of his system than to allow it to build up inside until there was a really big explosion that did some permanent damage?

The answer to this question is also negative. Mental health experts used to think that exploding was a far better alternative than imploding. In other words, they felt that if anger went unexpressed externally, people would damage themselves internally. They would begin to suffer the mental and emotional effects of bitterness and stress.

However, psychologists are now finding that venting anger actually increases hostility. A study by the American Psychological Association found that when people hit punching bags or other objects to relieve their anger, it actually increases their aggression. Hitting things seemed to give them some kind of permission to relax their self-control, and they began to experience anger more frequently and violently than before.[1] Psychologists have come to the conclusion that in the case of anger, self-control (one of the fruits that the Holy Spirit produces in our lives according to Galatians 5:23) is better than any form of aggressive self-expression.

So, should Ben have bottled up his anger and kept it inside himself?

No, that's not what I'm saying. Although most of the time anger should not be expressed, due to the damage that it would cause, it must always be dealt with. Anger is like that burning ember we just talked about. It is wrong to allow it to flare up and make toast out of all the people around us, but we shouldn't allow it to smolder inside where it will sear a hole right through our hearts either. We must learn to control it. A burning ember can destroy a whole forest if it is unrestrained. But when it is kept under control, it can give off heat that will warm us and provide light that can guide us.

IS ANGER EVER JUSTIFIED?

I am certainly not trying to convey that we should never feel angry. Anger is an emotion designed by God and deposited by Him into our beings. It is not a deviant feeling that arises only due to sin. We know this because the Bible recounts numerous instances of God's own anger. In Deuteronomy 4:25-26, He warned the Israelites of His fierce anger and informed them that He would wipe them out if they made idols for themselves. According to 2 Samuel 6:7, He was angry enough to kill a man named Uzzah for irreverently touching the Ark of the Covenant. And we know that even Jesus got angry. He lived a perfect, sinless life, yet He became so angry that He cleared out a whole temple courtyard with a whip when He found the Jewish leaders disgracing His Father's house (see John 2:14-16).

There are times God wants *us* to get angry, too. Righteous indignation in response to such injustices as racial prejudice, declining moral values, or the abuse of children can motivate us to do good things.

Do you remember how upset we were when we discovered that many of your friends from school did not participate in our youth baseball league because they could not afford the high registration fees and expensive equipment involved? It didn't seem fair that they couldn't play just because they came from families with low incomes. At first we were angry, but then we decided to do something about it. We recruited people who were willing to donate scholarships, we borrowed equipment, and we even got an optometrist to donate glasses for one little boy who couldn't see well enough to play.

No, anger is not always a deviant emotion that is a result of sin. But it *is* a response that must only be directed *at* sin. Anger is wrong when it is triggered by our selfishness or impatience. It becomes sin when it occurs because we value ourselves or the opinions of others more highly than we value the wisdom of God. Unfortunately, as we have already mentioned, about 99 percent of the time this is the case. Most often our anger occurs when we stop representing God, which is our duty as His children, and we start trying to represent ourselves — sticking up for who we think we are and demanding what we think we deserve.

HOW SHOULD I HANDLE MY ANGER?

Unrighteous anger can take several forms. But whether it displays itself often in short, frequent, outbursts like a Fourth of July sparkler, or in huge, infrequent explosions like dynamite, or constantly in long-simmering grudges, it is almost always a warning sign that something else is wrong. Just as the sharp pain that occurs when a grocery cart whacks you on the back of the ankle indicates that either the person behind you needs to slow down or you need to speed up, anger is a sign that either you or the situation you are involved in needs to change.

The first thing we need to do when we become aware of anger in our lives is to acknowledge that it is there. We must not try to redefine it as some reasonable expression based on our superiority or as an acceptable desire for justice. We must see it for what it really is and acknowledge that we are not reacting properly.

Often, if we look at it closely enough, we will discover that the anger we feel is due to the fact that we counted on other people to supply the happiness that only God can provide. When we find ourselves disappointed, unfulfilled, or hurt, we become angry. We need to refocus our attention and correct our opinion of God's love and sovereignty.

Next, we should figure out why we react in anger. An angry reaction is often influenced by what is modeled for us in our own homes or by our friends. Sometimes we copy the very behavior patterns we detest the most, because we feel it is justifiable in our situation. "If they can scream and holler when they are upset," we reason, "then I, being much more offended than they, certainly have earned the right to scream and holler or react aggressively when I'm upset." By putting up with their rage, we feel that we have earned the right to express our own.

Proverbs 22:24-25 says, "Do not make friends with a hot-tempered man, do not associate with one easily angered, or you may learn his ways and get yourself ensnared." We may need to step away from our friends and the situations that are filled with discontentment and hostility before they can further contaminate our lives.

Most important, we must release the anger, and the situation that surrounds it, to God. When we are willing to give up the right to have things go *our* way, anger cannot occur. Try it the next time your teacher announces an unscheduled test, or your best friend plans a trip to Disney World without you, or everyone else gets to go waterskiing and you have to baby-sit your little brother. Say, "God, I give up the right to be angry. I will not expect to always be exempt from the trials that other people have to endure." If you do this — if you give up the right to be angry — God can do wonderful things in your life. *God will change you!* It won't happen all at once, but if you give

Him the opportunity, He can turn tough times into triumphant ones. Listen to what David wrote in Psalm 37:5-8:

> Commit your way to the LORD; trust in him and he will do this: He will make your righteousness shine like the dawn, the justice of your cause like the noonday sun. Be still before the LORD and wait patiently for him; do not fret when men succeed in their ways, when they carry out their wicked schemes. Refrain from anger and turn from wrath; do not fret — it leads only to evil.

We must give away our anger — not by directing it at others, but by giving it to God. And we must do it today before the sun goes down! Ephesians 4:26-27 says, "Do not let the sun go down while you are still angry, and do not give the devil a foothold." God knows the damage that even one night of anger can cause. It can devastate relationships, destroy the quality of our personal lives, and damage our health. Doctors tell us that over 60 percent of all diseases are caused by emotional stress and much of that is due to anger. Anger causes the adrenal, thyroid, and pituitary glands to release toxins into our bloodstream that can lead to high blood pressure, strokes, heart attacks, ulcers, and many other fatal illnesses.[2]

If we allow anger to be our companion for even a single day, we also open ourselves to all kinds of attacks by Satan. Unresolved resentment gives Satan an entrance into our lives. Once inside, like cancer, his damaging grasp will spread. Like AIDS it will destroy our immune system, making us incapable of resisting sin.

Even a few minutes of anger can lead to devastation, because as Proverbs 14:17 tells us, "a quick-tempered man does foolish things." It took only one night of rage for my friend's brother to be locked behind bars for the rest of his life. He would give anything to relive the event that caused his anger. He would love to revise the reaction that took three lives.

When we give our anger to God instead of aiming it elsewhere, we are able to forgive. And forgiveness is like a cool drink on a hot day or like soothing aloe on a sunburn. It leaves us refreshed and revitalized. It stops the pain and allows healing to begin. In Ephesians 4:31-32 God tells us, "Get rid of all bitterness, rage and anger, brawling and slander, along with every form of malice. Be kind and compassionate to one another, forgiving each other, just as in Christ God forgave you."

People are inevitably going to hurt us. When someone else dates the person we love, or wins the nomination we were counting on, or spreads nasty rumors about us, it hurts! We must learn to grieve the damage or mourn our loss without reacting in anger. We must release the situation into God's hands. At the first sign of anger, we must be willing to forgive the person who caused the hurt. Forgiveness is a commitment to terminate any negative feelings that want to attach themselves to the pain.

Earlier in the book we talked about Joseph. If anyone ever had the right to harbor anger, he did. He was despised, bullied, abused, and sold into slavery by his older brothers. Later he was falsely accused of sexual assault, then selfishly forgotten and left to rot in a prison cell. Yet over and over he was able to set aside his anger and allow God to work through him. Years later when the very brothers who had initiated his journey of anguish and pain had to kneel before him to beg for food, he was able to speak his forgiveness. "Don't be afraid. Am I in the place of God?" he asked. "You intended to harm me, but God intended it for good to accomplish what is now being done, the saving of many lives. So then, don't be afraid. I will provide for you and your children." Then, the author of Genesis concluded, "He reassured them and spoke kindly to them" (Genesis 50:19-21).

Joseph was able to release any anger he might have felt toward his brothers to God. He didn't allow it to burn in his soul or explode in their presence. And God did greater things in his life than he ever could have imagined!

SUMMARY

The many changes taking place in your adolescent body and the turmoil of your teenage years leave you vulnerable to feelings of anger. But anger can be destructive. It can cause physical and emotional harm to your body and wreak havoc on your relationships. We must acknowledge any ungodly anger as the sin that it is rather than seek to justify it. We need to examine our surroundings to see if they may be influencing us to hold on to grudges. Then we must be willing to release our feelings to God. Releasing our anger requires forgiveness, which terminates our rights to harbor any negative feelings that have attached themselves to our pain. When we forgive those who hurt us, God is free to do marvelous things in and through us!

ISSUE #7

Where Is God When *I'm Afraid?*

Before any of you were born, Dad and I moved to Pine Cove Conference Center in east Texas. Dad was finishing his master's degree by commuting two and a half hours to Dallas twice every week. The trip was made worthwhile by the job opportunity offered at Pine Cove and the lovely surroundings it provided. But every once in a while the long commute made it necessary for Dad to spend the night in Dallas.

We lived in a mobile home nestled in an oak stand at one end of a very large horse pasture that rolled its way down to a shady lake. There could not have been a more beautiful setting. However, what was an idyllic location during the daylight hours could become very lonely and isolated once the sun went down.

When Dad was gone, it was very easy for nighttime loneliness to turn itself into fear. One night my *what-ifs* got the best of me. I double-bolted the door and placed all the furniture I could move in front of it. I figured if anyone tried to break in, they would at least have a little difficulty getting through. I also placed metal objects against the windows so they would clatter to the floor if anyone tried to open them. That night I stayed awake later than usual and spent extra time praying. I even asked God to send a special angel to protect me. Finally, sometime around 2:30 in the morning, weariness overtook my anxieties, and I fell asleep.

But about an hour later I was awakened by the sound of twigs snapping outside my bedroom window. I lay perfectly still, holding my breath as long as I could and hoping that I had just been imagining the noise.

Then I heard it again.

Rustle, rustle. Snap, snap.

This happened several times. Everything would be silent for about five minutes, then the leaves would rustle and the twigs would snap.

During that time my mind filled itself with a zillion *what-ifs.* I felt like my brain was about to explode. When the *what-ifs* started to obliterate reality, I knew I had to do something.

I threw off the covers, ran to the window, ripped open the curtains, and screamed at top of my lungs, hoping to scare the intruder more than he was scaring me.

I jumped back, startled. There, staring at me through the window was . . . a horse! He looked at me in a curious sort of way as if to say, "Hey lady, what's your problem?"

That was the first time I had ever seen a horse at our end of the pasture. I laughed and apologized for screaming at him and told him I would be grateful if he would spend the rest of the night outside the window protecting me. I don't know what his name was, but that night I renamed him Gabriel. I slept well knowing that God had indeed sent an angel (of sorts) to spend the night with me.

FOCUSING ON FAILURE LEADS TO FEAR

Thinking through negative possibilities can sometimes have positive results. It can prevent us from harming ourselves or causing injury to others. The fear of being involved in an automobile accident should always keep us from getting in the passenger seat of a car driven by someone who has been drinking. And fear of failure can motivate us to study when we otherwise might have blown off an exam. However, more often than not, the impact of fear is negative.

Fear is the consequence of a thought process that begins to alter the facts by adding possibilities. When we feel threatened, we begin to imagine possible outcomes for the situation. In order to protect ourselves from a devastating surprise, we immediately come up with negative scenarios. We picture ourselves failing in the form of embarrassment or rejection or isolation or physical harm. Often we tend to magnify the negative possibilities until we feel incapable of surviving the situation satisfactorily.

Let me illustrate this. Have you ever held up your hand to block out the sun? Does the fact that your hand can cover the sun completely mean that the sun is smaller than your hand? Of course not! The sun can still fit 1.3 million earths inside of it — and your hand can barely palm a basketball! Your hand only appears bigger than the sun because it is so much closer to you. In the same way, we sometimes focus so closely on our fears that they seem to block out God. We get so engrossed in our own inadequacies that we cannot see around them to focus on His power. He is just as big and powerful and awesome and loving as ever, but we are only able to see our own potential for failure rather than His promise of help.

Since fear is based on uncertainty rather than truth, it can result in irrational thoughts and behavior. None of my fears that lonely night in Texas were based on facts. They grew out of *what-ifs* that I allowed to invade my mind. They expanded rapidly, altering my perception of reality. I was quickly enveloped in unreasonable fear.

FOCUSING ON FEAR CAN CAUSE PARALYSIS

I'm sure that in one of your history classes you have heard of the stock market crash of 1929. It triggered the Great Depression and caused the darkest financial decade in American history. Over thirteen million people (one fourth of our working force) lost their jobs. Banks and businesses failed and financial institutions collapsed. In the midst of all this, Franklin Delano Roosevelt was elected President. In his first inaugural address on March 4, 1933, he boldly stated, "The only thing we have to fear is fear itself."

Roosevelt knew that fear has the power to paralyze. It can paralyze an individual, and because it is very contagious, it can paralyze a whole nation. When I was a young girl, I personally saw irrational fear paralyze an entire African village.

Late one afternoon, smack dab in the middle of the dry season, I noticed a man charging down the narrow lane that twisted through a shriveled grain field and led to our house. He dashed past the whitewashed, mud-brick church my father preached in and rushed into our yard. He hurried up the gravel path to our front porch ranting loudly in his native tongue and gesturing wildly with his hands. His eyes were as big as saucers and his gray beard quivered noticeably.

It took several minutes, but my father finally calmed him down enough to figure out that "giants" had invaded his village. They had come in the middle of the night, lifted the thatched roof off the granary bin, and stolen half of the villagers' precious grain supply.

The "giants," the man explained, had made off with their booty in round wooden pots that were so large and heavy that they had to stop and set them down every four or five feet. He described the huge, circular imprints that the villagers had found on the dusty ground. The "giants" had obviously rested from their heavy burdens by leaning against some small trees, uprooting them with their massive weight. Branches were strewn everywhere.

The man had been commissioned by the village chief to bring this message to my father, and it had taken him most of the day to make the journey. He begged my dad to come as soon as possible since no one in the village of about fifty huts could eat or sleep until the "giants" had been sufficiently persuaded never to return.

My father was intrigued by the story and decided to take off on his motorcycle and check out this "giant" invasion. Seeing the excitement in my eyes and the pleading look on my face, he allowed me to hop on behind him. I was ecstatic. I had seen God handle many unusual circumstances during my tenure as a missionary kid, but I had never seen Him handle "giants" before!

What followed was the wildest ride of my life. "Rhino Rally" at Busch Gardens offers nothing compared to that ride I took on the back of my dad's motorcycle. We were challenged by hyenas, bogged down in knee-deep sand, and threatened by impending darkness. The trail ended long before the trip to the village did, so for about five miles we wound our way through open fields and along dry riverbeds. At one point we hit a stump, which sent me sailing across a dusty field and sprawled me on top of an enormous anthill. We finally arrived with only minutes of daylight remaining.

The setting sun allowed just enough light for us to see the imprints that the "giants" had left behind with their huge wooden pots. My father smiled. I could tell that he was trying very hard not to burst out laughing. Kindly he explained that the tracks were not the evidence of huge "giants." They were the footprints of an elephant. Evidently a hungry female, separated from the herd, had sought food from the village granary. Along the way she had snacked on the saplings that lined the premises. The elephant had not caused much damage at all, but irrational fear had shut down the whole village.

The villagers marveled at my father's wisdom. Later they informed us that they slept well that night, leaving only one small boy on duty to ward off any other lost elephants that might lumber into town for a free meal.

Meanwhile my father and I slowly navigated our way back home through the darkness, across the sand, and past the hyenas with the aid of one very small flashlight and one very dim headlight. *No sweat!* I kept telling myself, as the shadows loomed large around us. *If God can handle "giants," He can handle this!*

FOCUSING ON FEAR CAN PROMPT WRONG RESPONSES

Our fears make the circumstances we are facing seem worse than they really are. We begin to imagine all that could go wrong, while forgetting to focus on all that God can do right. As we give in to our fears we strip ourselves of hope and rob ourselves of joy.

Satan loves for us to be afraid. When we yield to fear, we signal the fact that our faith is weak, and therefore we are susceptible to successful attack in other areas of our lives as well. Sometimes we allow fear to cloud our judgment and prompt us to do things we wouldn't ordinarily do or encourage us to participate in events we would normally avoid. We begin to rationalize the need to cheat in school or get in with the wrong crowd or go along with an unwise plan in order to prevent the consequences we have imagined.

Worst of all, accepting fear can cause us to miss out on the blessings that God has planned for us. The rich young ruler who desired the peace and joy of a relationship with God could not follow Jesus because he was too afraid to let go of his possessions. Perhaps he was afraid that life without them would be too tough. Or maybe he was afraid his friends would ridicule him. Obviously he was afraid that God wouldn't really take care of all his needs. I'm sure that his mind was filled with *what-ifs*. But regardless of its foundation, yielding to his fears kept him far from God and trapped him in sorrow (see Matthew 19:16-22).

Adam's response to fear caused him to hide in the bushes when God showed up for their evening walk (see Genesis 3:8-10). Surrendering to fear kept the children of Israel from entering the Promised Land when God first invited them to a home bursting with His blessings (see Numbers 13–14). Embracing their fears, instead of relying on their faith in a Savior who had performed countless miracles in their presence, kept cowardly disciples quivering in a wind-tossed boat when they could have been waltzing on the waves (see Matthew 14:22-33).

There are so many good times God wants to share with us and so many great things He wants to give us! But when we react on the basis of our fears we are unable to join Him. We can't reach out our hands and accept what He wants to give us when we are clinging to fear.

FEAR CAN BE PROVOKED BY OUR LIFESTYLE

Sometimes our fears are initiated or enlarged by the lifestyles we choose to live. If we watch scary shows on television or attend horrific movies filled with violence and abuse, we open ourselves to a barrage of fears. We need to screen the things we watch and monitor the songs we listen to and examine the topics we discuss with our friends so that we are not flirting with fear.

If you read the second book in this series, *Sticking Up for What Is Right,* you will recall that we discussed the fact that our minds are the workshops of the Holy Spirit (Dilemma #9). We should not allow unwholesome, intimidating thoughts to enter them and clutter up His workspace. The products of fear are nothing compared to the handiwork of the Holy Spirit (see Galatians 5:22-23).

FEAR CAN BE PROPERLY PLACED

"Hey, wait a minute," I hear you asking. "Doesn't the Bible say that 'the *fear* of the Lord is the beginning of wisdom'?"

Yes, it does — in Proverbs 1:7 and again in Proverbs 9:10. There is such a thing as healthy fear. Fear based on the power and character of a holy God who has every right to zap us into oblivion if we disobey Him can keep us from doing sinful things and motivate us to remain faithful. It can promote an attitude of awe and reverence and help us remember who we are compared to Who it is that sits on the throne of the universe ruling with wisdom and power beyond anything we can imagine. This kind of fear leads to faith.

Proper fear can keep us humble, and it can make us happy. Dozens of Scripture verses promise that God will protect and provide for those who fear Him. (Psalm 128:1-4 is one of these passages.) And the best thing about fearing God is that when we do, we have absolutely no reason to fear anything else! Did you get that? Let me say it again. When we fear God, we have absolutely no reason to fear anything else!

Have you ever read the prologue to the story of Moses found in Exodus 1:15-21? Shiphrah and Puah, two Hebrew midwives, were commanded by the Pharaoh of Egypt to kill all the baby boys who were born to the Hebrew women. But verse 17 says, "The midwives, however, *feared* God and did not do what the king of Egypt had told them to do; they let the boys live" (emphasis added).

When Pharaoh found out about this, he called the two women into his palace. I am sure their lives were on the line for their blatant disobedience of his command. There was huge potential for disaster and great cause for fear. But Shiphrah and Puah did not seem to be afraid of him at all. They defended their actions, and for some reason (directly related to God's sovereignty, I'm sure!) Pharaoh let them go.

Verses 20 and 21 conclude the story with this commentary: "So God was kind to the midwives and the people increased and became even more numerous. And because the midwives *feared* God, he gave them families of their own" (emphasis added).

"The remarkable thing about fearing God," wrote Oswald Chambers, a wonderful Bible teacher who lived from 1874–1917, "is that when you fear God, you fear nothing else, whereas if you do not fear God, you fear everything else."[1] The fear of God is both healthy and holy. But, to put it bluntly, giving in to any other kind of fear is sinful. It indicates that we are not trusting in God's wisdom or His power or His love. It is awfully hard for fear and faith to live in the same heart at the same time.

FEAR VANISHES WHEN WE FOCUS ON GOD'S STRENGTH

One fun summer we loaded up our van and headed north to visit friends and relatives. On the way home we stopped in Boone, North Carolina, and spent a few days sightseeing. I will never forget the afternoon we spent at Grandfather Mountain, the highest peak in the Blue Ridge Mountains. We were told that if we dared cross a long suspension bridge called Mile-High Swinging Bridge, we could stand on a rocky ledge that offers a tremendous (and unfenced — I might add!) view of the valley thousands of feet below.

It was late afternoon when we arrived at the bridge, and a storm was blowing in. The wind was beginning to gust significantly. I took one look down the eighty-foot-deep ravine spanned by the bridge, clutched baby Jonathan, and refused to set foot on it. But before I could restrain the rest of you, Zach and MattE took off running. You were about halfway across the swaying boards when the wind became so strong it made you stagger. But you loved the challenge and the thrill and fought your way to the other side. Ben, who had started running after you, stopped suddenly and clung to the nearest post. He was only three years old and wasn't so sure he wanted to continue the dangerous trek.

Dad, seeing what fun Zach and MattE were having as they fought against the wind, reached for Ben's hand and said, "Let's go. I'll take care of you."

It was obvious that all kinds of *what-ifs* started tumbling around inside Ben's mind as he stood glued to the post contemplating Dad's offer. But suddenly he reached up, grabbed Dad's big hand, and started skipping across the bridge into the gusting wind. Ben had obviously transferred all of his *what-ifs* to Dad and decided to let him worry about them. The swaying bridge, the extreme height, the blustery wind, the impending storm — these weren't his problems anymore. Whether or not *he* could handle the situation did not matter. It was completely Dad's responsibility.

We need to do the same thing with our *what-ifs*. Regardless of the situation causing our anxiety, we need to transfer our fears to God and allow Him to be responsible for working out the details of our safety and care. Facing fear provides us with a tremendous opportunity to exercise our faith.

Instead of focusing on the *what-ifs*, we need to focus on *what is! What is* includes the fact that God knows every detail of every situation that produces anxiety in our lives. He is never caught by surprise or unprepared to handle even the most catastrophic event that suddenly interrupts our plans. Nor is He oblivious to the most mundane moments in our everyday routine.

What is involves the fact that God is powerful enough to change our circumstances if He chooses to. God never wrings His hands in despair and says, *"Oh no, this wasn't supposed to happen!"* Everything that takes place, from a baby catching a cold to a huge volcano blowing its lid, is subject to His control.

What is also contains the fact that God loves us. He loves us enough to do whatever is best for us. However, His reasoning isn't always the same as ours. For instance, I don't think God would find Himself thinking: *MattE forgot to study last night. However, if he doesn't pass this algebra test, he might not get into the college I want him to go to. Therefore, I guess I'd better miraculously slip the answers into his brain—especially since he's praying so hard!* God knows MattE's situation and He has the power to intervene in any way He chooses. But He also loves MattE enough to teach him the importance of studying and fulfilling his responsibilities. God sometimes allows us to suffer the consequences of our poor choices so that we will learn important lessons. But God *always* loves us enough to do what is best.

First Peter 5:7 tells us to cast all our anxieties on God because He cares for us. Based on His knowledge, power, and love, we must give our fears to God—just as Ben handed his fears to Dad that day on Grandfather Mountain. God wants to hold our hands so that we can skip into the wind and enjoy it rather than be frightened or paralyzed by it.

SUMMARY

Fear is the consequence of a thought process that begins to alter the facts by adding possibilities. It occurs when we allow our minds to manufacture and magnify possible outcomes that are less than desirable. Giving in to fear can paralyze us. It can cloud our judgment and prompt us to do things we wouldn't ordinarily do, or participate in events we would normally stay away from. Worst of all, by submitting to fear we miss out on the blessings that God has planned for us.

Regardless of the situation that triggered our fear, we need to transfer it to God and allow Him to be responsible for working out the details of our safety and care. Instead of focusing on the *what-ifs*, we need to start focusing on *what is!* We need to relax in God's knowledge, rest in His power, and rejoice in His love. Fear (other than the fear of God) and faith cannot live in the same heart at the same time.

ISSUE #8

WHY CAN LIFE BE SO DECENT *One Day, Then So Discouraging the Next?*

IT WAS A TRADITION AT ZACH AND MATTE'S HIGH SCHOOL FOR THE GRADuating class to present a gift to the school as a remembrance of their years in attendance. Accompanying this honorable tradition was another, much less honorable one. Most years the senior guys took it upon themselves to leave another tribute in the form of a prank just a few days before graduation.

Everyone remembers the year when all the old oak trees that separated the classrooms from the football field were "rolled" with toilet paper. For a week it looked like giant cones of white cotton candy had descended from the sky. Rumor has it that another year pranksters escorted a cow up the outside steps and onto the second floor balcony. Although cows willingly climb stairs, evidently they are adamantly opposed to going back down. A frightened cow can make quite a mess all over a six-foot-wide balcony in the course of one night!

The year MattE graduated, however, a few of the guys took the tradition several steps too far. They broke into the school and poured motor oil down one of the hallways and on several lockers. Their prank caused serious damage and was quite dangerous because the oil was flammable. Fortunately the police caught them before they carried their plans any further.

After lengthy deliberations, the administration decided not to press criminal charges. Instead they decided to punish the offenders by not allowing them to "walk" with the graduating class. Although they would later receive their diplomas, they were told that they would have to watch the ceremony from the audience with their parents.

The punishment caused a great debate. Several parents of the offenders were irate. They felt that the penalty was far too harsh and unfair. Then some of the senior class leaders decided to boycott the graduation ceremonies. They demanded a meeting with the administration to reinstate their friends in the procession. Wisely, the principal decided to hold a town meeting with all of the faculty and senior students in attendance.

At the meeting, the administration stated their case and then several of the seniors spoke up in disagreement—quite vociferously, I am told! Repeatedly they emphasized that *everyone* in the senior class wanted the boys to take part in the graduation ceremonies and that *no one* felt that they deserved the penalty that had been assessed.

Evidently, at one point you stood up, MattE, and slowly began to explain that you understood why many of your classmates did not agree with the punishment. However, you wanted them to know that not *everyone* in the class agreed with their evaluation—because *you*, for one, did not. You knew you could not speak for anyone else, but you felt that putting the student body at risk and causing hundreds of dollars worth of damage required some kind of consequence. You admitted that over the course of your high school years you had been taught many lessons based on the consequences of your behavior. You felt that the guys (some of them your friends) should be willing to accept the penalty and be grateful that it was not worse.

The room was silent. You knew that many of your classmates felt the same way you did, but they were too intimidated to back you up at the time. The meeting soon adjourned, and buoyed by your support, the administration decided to keep the penalty in place.

On the way out of the room, the faculty and staff thanked you for daring to stand up and speak the truth in love. As a matter of fact, so did many of your classmates. You knew you had done the right thing, and you felt very good about it — for about ten minutes!

That's when everything seemed to fall apart, and you began to wish you had never opened your mouth. Led by the boys who had been the perpetrators of the prank, you were labeled a traitor and a snitch. You were threatened and alienated by many of your former "friends." Life became miserable. Fewer and fewer classmates stood by your side. The fact that you had just led your baseball team into the regional finals and had been elected prom king by the student body a few weeks earlier suddenly meant nothing. Those last few days of high school were pretty gloomy, weren't they, MattE?

How could doing something so right result in such a catastrophe? How could someone's status in life fluctuate so quickly? One moment you were floating on top of the world like a brightly colored, helium-filled balloon and the very next, you were stuck on a barbed, wire fence tattered and deflated. You were discouraged for weeks.

Over and over in the Bible we are given examples of godly people who experienced great victory one day, then found themselves in the depths of discouragement and defeat the next. Shortly after the miraculous crossing of the Red Sea and the destruction of Pharaoh's army, and not long after spending time with God Himself on Mount Sinai, Moses found himself begging God to take his life (see Numbers 11:15). After the greatest revival recorded in Scripture, Jonah sat down at the edge of town and sulked. He pleaded with God just to go ahead and let him die (see Jonah 4:3). One minute Peter was used by God to reveal that Jesus was indeed "the Christ, the Son of the living God" and the next he became the tool of Satan (see Matthew 16:16-23). After many miraculous moments with God, things got so bad that the great apostle Paul "despaired even of life" (see 2 Corinthians 1:8). It is safe to say that no one is exempt from times of great discouragement. But what is it that brings on such despair, and how can we learn to handle it?

DISCOURAGING TIMES TEND TO FOLLOW TIMES OF GREAT SUCCESS

The prophet Elijah had an experience that can teach us a lot about discouragement. According to the account in 1 Kings 18, Elijah challenged 450 prophets of Baal to a contest to determine whose god was the greatest — the God of the Israelites or the god of Baal. Who would be the winner? The god who had the power to send fire from the sky and burn up an offering made on his behalf.

The day of the contest began early on the summit of Mount Carmel. First the prophets of Baal built their stone altar. They stacked wood on top, then sacrificed a bull. They prayed to their god, Baal, entreating him to send fire to consume their sacrifice. From morning until night they screamed and begged and danced and even cut their own bodies trying to gain his favor. But he failed to respond.

Then it was Elijah's turn. He repaired an old altar, cut wood, and sacrificed his bull. But he wasn't ready for God to send fire just yet. Adding a little more drama to the event, he filled four large containers with water and then poured them onto his sacrifice. (This was a lot harder than it sounds. The whole nation was in the middle of a severe drought, and any water they used had to be hauled clear up the mountain.) Three times Elijah commanded this to be done until the entire altar was soaked and the trenches around it were completely full.

> [Then] Elijah stepped forward and prayed: "O LORD, God of Abraham, Isaac and Israel, let it be known today that you are God in Israel and that I am your servant and have done all these things at your command. Answer me, O LORD, answer me, so these people will know that you, O LORD, are God, and that you are turning their hearts back again." Then the fire of the LORD fell and burned up the sacrifice, the wood, the stones and the soil, and also licked up the water in the trench (1 Kings 18:36-38).

Elijah's God, the God of the Israelites, had clearly won the contest. The people, realizing that the prophets of Baal had lied to them for years, revolted against them. They captured all 450 prophets and killed them in the valley below. Then, as a tremendous rainstorm broke the drought, Elijah miraculously outran the chariots of King Ahab down the mountain to safety.

Wow! What a day for Elijah! He (with God's help) had single-handedly defeated the prophets of Baal and then outrun the fastest horses in the nation! There could not have been a more dramatic or conclusive victory, and the power of God could not have been publicized from a greater place than the top of Mount Carmel. Elijah must have been feeling great by the time he got ready for bed!

But in the very next chapter we find Elijah huddled under a scrub tree in the desert, wanting to die. In a matter of hours his tremendous victory seemed futile. Four hundred and fifty yelling and screaming prophets hadn't even come close to disheartening him, but the whispered threat of a wicked lady left him in despair (see 1 Kings 19:1-5).

It is difficult for us to sustain mountaintop experiences for very long. A step in any direction is likely to land us a little lower than we were before. One of the problems is that once we reach a summit, our tendency is to relax and lose our focus. How often during your baseball careers have you guys been on a team that pulled off a huge victory against a much more prestigious team and then lost the very next game to a ragamuffin squad you should have easily defeated?

Elijah didn't seem to understand that the battle was not over at Mount Carmel. It had really just begun. He had seen God's great display of divine power, but he forgot to focus on God's constant presence.

God doesn't just show up for the "big events" in our lives. He promises that He will *never* leave us or forsake us (see Hebrews 13:5). It is only our choice to ignore Him that causes His presence to seem less obvious. The intimidating threats that were whispered from the lips of Queen Jezebel were no more challenging to God than the feeble shrieks of the prophets of Baal. But they disheartened Elijah because he suddenly felt obligated to deal with them on his own. Let's learn from some of the things that contributed to Elijah's discouragement and despair.

WE TEND TO BE EASILY DISCOURAGED WHEN WE ARE PHYSICALLY EXHAUSTED

Elijah's experience on Mount Carmel no doubt left him weak and worn out. Spending a full day on a mountaintop in the sun and wind can be draining with nothing else going on, but Elijah also experienced the stress of a major conflict followed by a long, grueling run down a steep, rocky hill. He probably hadn't stopped to eat all day either. By the time the bull on his altar caught fire, he didn't have time to stick around and enjoy a roast beef sandwich! There was much more work for him to do. There were prophets to execute and prayers to be made. By the time Elijah had finished his responsibilities, it was getting dark and a storm was blowing in. He had to get off the mountain quickly, and he didn't have the luxury of owning a chariot.

Elijah hardly had time to catch his breath from his marathon run when he heard the threats of Queen Jezebel (see 1 Kings 19:2). And guess what — he took off running again. By the time he found a broom tree in the desert to hide beneath, he was so depleted and exhausted that he begged God to take his life. He was in such despair that he couldn't stand the thought of living even one more day. Before he could utter another word, he fell fast asleep.

WE TEND TO BE EASILY DISCOURAGED WHEN WE FORGET WHAT GOD LOOKS LIKE

Elijah made the mistake of taking his eyes off the God who had just trounced 450 prophets of Baal with His miraculous power. Instead he allowed himself to focus on one wicked lady. Next to God, she was nothing. But without God in the picture, she seemed meaner than a monster with a migraine. When he neglected to include God's power and love in the picture, Elijah was no match for Queen Jezebel. Instead of smiling at the thought of one little lady standing up to an almighty God, he found himself trembling under a scrub tree imagining himself as good as gone.

WE TEND TO BE EASILY DISCOURAGED WHEN WE FEEL EMOTIONALLY ABANDONED

Not only was Elijah exhausted and unfocused, he was lonely. The next time he talked to God, he began to complain about his situation. "I have been so zealous for you, God!" he pouted. "As a matter of fact, I'm the only one left who is standing up for You. There is not a single person in this whole nation serving You except me. Yet You are allowing me to be persecuted! Oh, poor me, I am not only unappreciated, I'm all alone."

Elijah felt that he was carrying the whole weight of God's work on his shoulders. But God quickly filled him in on the facts. He wasn't alone at all. There were actually seven *thousand* others in Israel who had not bowed to Baal, and God named three men who would step in and take Elijah's place (see 1 Kings 19:15-18).

HOW CAN WE CONQUER DISCOURAGEMENT?

You may come to a point in your life when you are filled with despair and desperation, just as Elijah was. But God does not want you to become trapped by the miserable circumstances that took you there. He will rescue you—just as He rescued Elijah—if you will let Him. God began a three-step process in Elijah's life that brought him out of his despondency and restored him to active, exciting service. It is the same process that He wants to apply to our lives whenever we become discouraged or depressed.

1. We need to get the rest and physical care our bodies require.

While Elijah was sleeping under the broom tree, God sent an angel to bake him a very special cake (ever heard of "angel food cake"?) and supply him with some bottled water. After he ate, Elijah went back to sleep again. When he woke up and ate again he was finally rested and refreshed. He was strong enough to go on a special retreat where he could spend time rediscovering God's power and love.

The status of our emotional lives is very dependent on our physical condition. We are most vulnerable to depression when we are physically drained. So one of the first things we need to do when life begins to feel dark and depressing is make sure we are getting the rest and nourishment that our bodies need. Lack of sleep limits our ability to think and act rationally. It causes us to make inaccurate evaluations and unwise decisions. It can trigger anger and fear, because when we are tired we have difficulty controlling our emotions. Lack of sleep leaves our bodies more susceptible to illness and our minds less capable of concentration.

Because of the rapid growth and chemical changes taking place in your body, you require even *more* sleep as a teenager than you did as an elementary school student. Your bodies actually require about nine hours of sleep each night if they are going to perform adequately! (I didn't make this up! I found it mentioned in several different medical magazines.) You can function for a while with less sleep, but you will accumulate a sleep deficit that can eventually lead to emotional or mental problems.

And the food you eat supplies the energy you need to carry out all the activities you are involved in without becoming weak or ill. It is important for you to eat breakfast before leaving for school and to eat nourishing foods at lunchtime and dinner if you want to stay healthy. Getting enough physical exercise is also important to prevent discouragement and depression. God understands our emotional needs better than anyone else. After all, He is the one who designed us! And the first thing He did for Elijah when he was discouraged and depressed was make sure his physical needs were met.

2. We need to keep our eyes on God rather than the difficult situation. After supplying Elijah with the food and rest he needed, God once again demonstrated His power and love so that Elijah would keep trusting Him. He revealed His strength in ways that Elijah would never forget (see 1 Kings 19). He tore the mountains apart with a mighty wind. He shook the rocks with an earthquake. And He consumed all that remained with a fire. Then God expressed His love and His plan through a gentle whisper that was meant only for the ears of one man — Elijah. Never again did Elijah take his eyes off God.

Do you remember the ropes course at the camp we used to visit whenever we went to Texas? One of the obstacles you had to overcome was a twenty-four-foot-long narrow board that crossed a deep gully. Because you were always competing against another person or team, you had to cross from the platform on one side to the platform on the other as quickly as possible without falling into the little stream that trickled below. Not only would you get muddy and dirty if you fell off, you would probably keep your team from winning! Sometimes the gully looked very deep and your feet felt very insecure.

Although it didn't seem to make much sense, the counselors insisted that it was much easier to cross the board if you did not look down at your feet. They claimed that you would be much less likely to wobble and fall if you looked straight ahead at your destination — the platform on the other side. It was difficult to stay focused, but the campers who took the counselors' advice were always the ones who crossed the most quickly and easily — and rarely did they land in the muck.

One of the only ways we can make it through life without slipping and falling into despair is to keep our eyes on God. We will not make it if we focus on ourselves. We are no match for the temptations and trials that confront us every day. If we compare our strength with the situations we are facing and fail to include God's power in the equation, we will easily become defeated. If we try to make it on our own without listening for God's loving voice, we will quickly become discouraged. Rather than seeking answers from God for the difficulties we face, it is more important for us to seek God Himself. We need to find quiet places where we can read the Bible and pray and listen to God as He makes Himself known to us.

3. We need a friend who will help us when life gets heavy.

After making it very clear to Elijah that he was not alone, God gave him a partner. Elisha became his assistant, and for the rest of Elijah's life on earth, the two of them shared the blessings and burdens of the ministry. Elisha became a tremendous source of camaraderie and strength for Elijah.

Do you remember playing in the gravel near the dam that Uncle Bill helped engineer in Pennsylvania? The first thing you did when we arrived was slide down a little hill into one of the pits. You had a blast playing in the gravel, enjoying the dirt as only little boys can. But when you got tired of playing and wanted to join us up by the dam, you discovered that you couldn't get out. You could run about halfway up the embankment, but then the loose gravel would start a little avalanche and you would slide right back down to the bottom. Over and over you tried until you were totally exhausted and lay in a heap at the bottom. Finally (after teasing you about your predicament), Uncle Bill and Dad reached down, grabbed your hands, and pulled you out of the pit.

Well, that's what happened to Elijah, and often it happens to us. We slip into pits and find ourselves trapped — unable to get out on our own. We start to panic and begin to feel desperate. That's when we need the encouragement of a companion. We need someone to come along and give us a hand just as Elijah needed Elisha. Ecclesiastes 4:9-10 says, "Two are better than one, because they have a good return for their work: If one falls down, his friend can help him up." We need to hook up with friends or family members or church leaders who know God and who can help us refocus on Him when we find ourselves focusing on our problems.

And sometimes we need to seek the support of professionals. Counselors and psychologists have been trained to help people who have become so entangled by despair that the only way out seems to be through self-destruction. If you ever find yourself contemplating injury or suicide as a means of escaping your desperate circumstances, you must immediately reach out to a trained professional. Any church or hospital or school can refer you to one. There are times when each of us may need a special hand to cling to. Elijah sure did!

Don't ever give up hope. Just look at what God did for Elijah! In 2 Kings 1 we find the same man who had been so afraid of Jezebel that he wanted to die, sitting on top of a hill challenging whole battalions of soldiers to just try to touch him! He no longer feared anyone. He knew God would protect him.

God wants to rescue and protect us, too. And He will, if we will let Him. Discouraging times are inevitable, but they are not inescapable!

SUMMARY

Not one of us is immune from tumbling into the depths of discouragement. Almost all of the great men and women in the Bible at some time found themselves struggling with despair. From their lives we learn that times of great discouragement often follow times of great success. This is particularly evident in the life of Elijah. We learn from his experience that we can easily become discouraged when we are physically exhausted. Just as God refreshed Elijah with food and rested him from his weariness, we need to be sure our bodies receive the food and sleep and physical exercise that they need in order to avoid discouragement. It is hard to respond with wholesome emotions when our bodies are physically depleted.

One of the quickest ways to become discouraged is to take our eyes off God. We must constantly center our focus on His power and love. We learn from Elijah how vital it is to have companions who will help us through the difficult times and keep us from becoming trapped by discouragement.

ISSUE #9

If God Loves Me, Why Does *He Let Me Hurt?*

Six-year-old Ben came bursting into the house. Tears were streaming down his face. "Come quick! I think I broke Jonathan's arm," he bawled. (I'm still not sure if he was feeling genuine sorrow for his little brother, or experiencing the remorse that precedes the possibility of punishment.)

Three-year-old Jonathan followed him into the house clutching a limp right arm. There were no tears, but his face was white with pain. One look at his arm left no doubt. It was not just broken — it was shattered. There was a puffy, s-shaped curve just below his elbow.

That morning all four of you had been particularly full of life. I had sent you outside to play before you left for school so that you would not drive your teachers nuts with your excess energy. Ben had decided to give Jonathan a "riding lesson." He helped his younger brother onto the little red bike with the training wheels and pushed him off down our neighbor's long driveway. Then Ben hopped on his two-wheeler and followed closely behind. Everything was going great until Jonathan hit a bump in the pavement that sent him crashing to the ground. As he sprawled across the cement, Ben accidentally ran over his outstretched arm.

Both of the bones in Jonathan's lower arm were fractured. One of them broke all the way through, but the other remained partially intact. The good news was that the treatment did not require surgery—the orthopedic surgeon was able to set the bones in his office. The bad news was that the process was very painful. The second bone had to be broken completely before the doctor could fix the arm correctly. Because he was dealing with such a young patient, the surgeon decided to use only local anesthesia. Many years later, Jonathan vividly recalls that excruciating moment when "the doctor snapped my arm in half!"

This is certainly not the most traumatic event that has ever happened to a three-year-old. Nor is it the most traumatic event that has taken place in Jonathan's life. But it does raise a question: Why does God allow us to experience pain? What purpose does a broken arm serve in a three-year-old's life? Why should a teenager have to encounter the emotional grief of not "fitting in" at school, or an elderly person endure declining health? Why should a parent face the agony of her child dying, or a factory worker undergo the stress of losing a job? What about all the mental, physical, and emotional abuse that goes on in our society? These are difficult questions we have to answer while clinging to our faith in God.

We discussed the origin of pain and suffering quite thoroughly in Question #3 of *Sticking Up for What I Believe.* We discovered that God did not create pain or suffering. They entered the world as a result of Adam's choice to disobey God's commandments. With them came the reality of spending all of eternity separated from God in a constant state of pain. We found that according to

2 Peter 3:9, God allows the suffering here on earth to continue so that as many people as possible can be given the opportunity to accept Jesus Christ as their Savior and escape the horrors of an eternity without God.

God is not powerless to get rid of pain. He is just patient. He wants as many people as possible to have a chance to accept His offer of salvation. But God has promised that someday He will completely do away with all evil on this planet and annihilate all the pain it causes. Then we, who have chosen to accept the sacrifice of His Son, will live forever in an eternally perfect world free from all suffering! Wow, what an exciting future we have to look forward to!

Meanwhile we find ourselves living in a world that includes hardship and pain. Some of it is a result of poor choices that we make. For example, if you choose not to study, you will probably get bad grades. If you choose to drink and drive, you will likely become a statistic in an accident report. If you choose to eat poorly or abuse your body, you will be much more susceptible to illness and injury.

But many times the bad things that come into our lives are *not* caused by our own shortcomings. It wasn't Jonathan's fault that his arm was broken. He wasn't doing anything wrong (that morning!). And it wasn't Ben's fault either. Ben was actually trying to be a wonderful big brother.

Many people suffer through no fault of their own. It wasn't Andy's fault that his parents decided they couldn't live together after fifteen years. It wasn't Miguel's responsibility that the rest of his family was killed in a mudslide several years ago. And Margaret did nothing to deserve the asthmatic attacks that put her in the hospital several times a year. To put it in baseball terminology, sometimes you can make a great pitch and still get "lit up."

TOUGH STUFF HAPPENS TO EVERYONE

In John 16:33, Jesus warns us that we are all going to face painful times in our lives — not because we do bad things, but just because we live in this world. He puts it this way, "In this world you will have trouble. But take heart! I have overcome the world."

Tough stuff is going to come into our lives. There is no way we can escape it — and no one is exempt! Our job is to expect God to help us through the pain when it arrives and to allow Him to use it however He chooses. We can even experience joy in the midst of the pain knowing that Jesus has already won the battle for us. James tells us that we will eventually wear a crown of victory if we persevere through the trials we face (see James 1:12).

In the book of Esther we are told the story of a young girl who faced a terribly painful childhood yet experienced great victory and found herself wearing a crown — literally! Esther had three major strikes against her in life. First, she was Jewish, and the entire Jewish nation had been conquered by the Babylonians. Everyone had either been killed or captured. As prisoners of war, they had been taken into exile in Babylon and forced to adapt to foreign customs and adopt foreign gods. Those who resisted were arrested. (Do you remember the story of Shadrach, Meshach, and Abednego in Daniel 3? They were thrown into a fiery furnace when they refused to worship a golden image of the king.)

Because of her Jewish heritage Esther was able to enjoy very little freedom. But not only was she Jewish — Esther was a female. That was the second strike against her. Even in a free society, she would have had very few privileges because most of the civil rights at that time in history belonged to the males. A woman's rights were those granted to her by her husband or father.

The third devastating strike against Esther was the fact that both her parents had died. In that society, an orphaned young girl was the most destitute of all people with very little hope of improving her status. She had nothing to offer the family of a young Jewish man in exchange for the right to marry him. The only thing Esther had going for her was the fact that she was drop-dead gorgeous. But that didn't count for much. She had no property, no possessions, no power or prestige — nothing that would attract another family to promise their son to her in marriage. She had no way to support herself and very little chance of ever getting married or bearing children.

Through no fault of her own, Esther endured a very painful childhood and could only look forward to a pitiful adulthood. She had very little freedom, very few rights, and almost no hope. And you can add to her horrible condition the fact that a deranged and detestable man who hated the Jews had risen to power and convinced the king to issue an edict demanding their annihilation!

But God had a purpose for the pain that Esther endured. Everything that made her unattractive to a Jewish family in search of a spouse for their son made her available for God's plan. If she had been engaged to a young Jewish man, as most girls her age would have been, she never would have been eligible to enter the beauty pageant the king conducted in his search for a new wife. Not only was she chosen to participate — she won the whole thing! Talk about a crown of victory! (see James 1:12). Esther was given the most prestigious crown any girl on earth could have worn at that time in history. She became the queen of Persia! And she took on this powerful, prestigious position at the perfect moment to save her people from extermination. God used Esther to rescue the entire Jewish nation!

God always has a purpose for the pain that He permits to enter our lives. If He can't use it, He won't allow it. Let's discuss some of the reasons God allows us to experience pain.

SOMETIMES GOD ALLOWS US TO EXPERIENCE PAIN IN ORDER TO PROTECT US

God doesn't sit up in heaven waiting to zap us when we do something wrong. But God sometimes uses pain to get our attention. He wants to protect us in the same way that parents want to protect their children. He will allow us to suffer a temporary injury if He knows it can prevent us from sustaining permanent damage.

When you were little, if you reached your fingers toward the stove or an electrical socket, we would not only remove you from the harmful situation, we would often smack your little hands. We did this because we knew that the minor pain we inflicted could keep you from major pain later on. Well, God disciplines us in the same way. Hebrews 12:6-7,10-11 says:

> "The Lord disciplines those he loves, and he punishes everyone he accepts as a son." Endure hardship as discipline; God is treating you as sons. For what son is not disciplined by his father? . . . God disciplines us for our good, that we may share in his holiness. No discipline seems pleasant at the time, but painful. Later on, however, it produces a harvest of righteousness and peace for those who have been trained by it.

God used a shoulder injury to show a friend of ours who is a major league catcher that there is more to life than fame and fortune and parties. During his painful rehabilitation, he recognized that the sport on which he had staked so much of his life couldn't provide satisfaction or security. He realized that if he relied on baseball for his fulfillment, he was in for a pretty meaningless life. God led several people across his path who explained to him that true fulfillment can only be found in a relationship with Jesus Christ. One day not long ago he got down on his knees and accepted Jesus Christ as his Savior. But it took the physical pain of the injury and the emotional pain of losing what he thought he loved most, before God was able to capture his attention.

SOMETIMES GOD ALLOWS US TO EXPERIENCE PAIN IN ORDER TO PRUNE US

Just before spring arrives each year, Dad goes "clipper crazy." You know what I mean. On a bright sunny Saturday he heads into the yard with a ladder, an electric trimmer, and the long pruning pole. He spends the better part of the day cutting things. He trims the hedges, hacks back the palm trees, scalps the azalea bushes, lops off limbs from the oak trees, and basically prunes everything growing in the yard. (The dog has to hide or he would lose his tail!) You guys can think of a million things you'd rather do on a sunny Saturday in March, but you're stuck hauling off branches and trimmings until he is done. I remember one time MattE yelling, "Come on, Dad, quit killing things!"

But the truth is, Dad isn't killing things. The things he prunes are much more full and shapely and productive after they are trimmed than they would have been if left to grow on their own. And that's what God does with us. When He sees an area in our life that is getting a little scraggly, He often cuts it back so that it will be able to produce more fruit. In John 15:1-2, Jesus says, "I am the true vine, and my Father is the gardener. He cuts off every branch in me that bears no fruit, while every branch that does bear fruit he prunes so that it will be even more fruitful."

God does not want us to settle for mediocre, shriveled fruit in our lives. He knows that only the fruit produced by the Holy Spirit will bring us true happiness. He wants to yield a bumper crop of "love, joy, peace, patience, kindness, goodness, faithfulness, gentleness and self-control" in our lives (Galatians 5:22-23).

SOMETIMES GOD ALLOWS US TO EXPERIENCE PAIN IN ORDER TO REVEAL HIS POWER AND GLORY

God used the pain Esther experienced early in her life to magnificently reveal His power to the world. This is also true of the physical and emotional pain suffered by the blind man whose story is found in John 9. (We talked about him in Issue #3.) When Jesus' disciples asked, "Rabbi, who sinned, this man or his parents, that he was born blind?" Jesus answered, "Neither this man nor his parents sinned . . . but this happened so that the work of God might be displayed in his life" (John 9:2-3). And the death of Lazarus, the brother of Mary and Martha, made it possible for Jesus' disciples and those around them to "see the glory of God" (John 11:40). We'll talk more about this incident later in the chapter.

When I was in high school my dad became very ill. He could no longer work or support our family in any way. This left us with very little money for food or clothing. And it left me with very little hope of attending college. Yet God had other plans for my life. Just as in Esther's story, He took a situation that looked devastating by human standards and gave it divine dimensions. Through a wonderful maze of God-planned events, He presented me with a full scholarship to an Ivy League university where I not only received a valuable education, but also met and married the man who became your father. It wasn't my grades or my good deeds that got me into that college. It was my poverty!

You see, each year the University of Pennsylvania distributed several scholarships designated only for destitute high school graduates from poor rural communities. (The fact that I was a female further enhanced my chances of receiving one.) The poverty, which could have brought great pain into my life, produced invaluable lessons concerning God's divine protection and remarkable love.

SOMETIMES GOD ALLOWS US TO EXPERIENCE PAIN IN ORDER TO SPREAD THE GOSPEL

After His resurrection, Jesus Christ appeared to His followers and commanded them to spread the good news all over the world. However, instinctively they huddled together in Jerusalem for safety and support. It took a little heat in their lives to get them to comply with Christ's commands.

One day a religious leader named Saul (who later became the great apostle Paul) began dragging Christians out of their homes and imprisoning them. He then stood and watched as one of them, Stephen, was stoned to death. Acts 8:1 says, "On that day a great persecution broke out against the church at Jerusalem, and all except the apostles were scattered throughout Judea and Samaria." The Christians in Jerusalem ran for their lives!

Some people refer to it as the Spiritual Law of Thermodynamics — when the heat increased, the church expanded! It wasn't pleasant for the disciples to experience painful persecution, but it was necessary to get them to leave Jerusalem and take the message of Jesus' resurrection to the places God intended for it to go.

During the years I lived in Africa I watched my father tackle many medical emergencies. I think his only qualification as a health worker came from a first aid course he had taken many years before. But supplied with a little bit of medicine and an assortment of odd equipment, he was called on to treat everything from leprosy to lime disease; from decayed teeth to infected toenails; from yellow fever to pinkeye.

One of the most challenging medical assignments he faced was removing the top of a fifty-gallon gasoline drum from the upper arm of a small boy. Evidently the lad had dropped something down the hole in the large container and had reached inside to retrieve it. When he tried to remove his arm, he could not get his elbow back through the opening. The more he struggled the more swollen his arm became.

Several men in his village tried to free him, but all their efforts failed. Their last hope was to amputate his arm. But just before they did, someone suggested that they cut the lid from the drum and carry him (with the lid still attached to his arm) to my father. By the time they made the journey to our house, the little boy's arm was grotesquely distended, and he was in agony.

The only piece of equipment my father owned that could cut through the metal was a hacksaw. But using it near the swollen arm was dangerous. It took several hours, but with one man holding the boy still, another maneuvering a thin sheet of wood between the saw blade and the flesh of the boy's arm, and my mother pouring a steady stream of cold water to reduce the swelling and the heat from the friction, my father finally removed the metal ring.

It was a painful experience for that young child, but God had a divine purpose. Extremely grateful for his help, the men were willing to listen to the message my dad had traveled all the way to Africa to share. They invited him back to their village to tell the story of God's love. Dozens of people will spend their eternities in heaven because God chose to use the predicament of that little boy to spread the gospel.

Painful experiences are inevitable in our lives. God allows them for several reasons. Sometimes they protect us; sometimes they prune us; sometimes they display God's power; and sometimes they spread the message of His love. But how are we supposed to react when we find ourselves hurting?

WE MUST NOT MISTAKE THE PRESENCE OF PAIN FOR THE ABSENCE OF GOD

When Lazarus became ill, his sisters immediately sent for Jesus. He was their friend, and He had often stayed in their home in Bethany. If Mary and Martha had never seen Him demonstrate His healing power in the busy synagogues or along the dusty lanes of Israel, they certainly had heard many stories of the miracles He had performed. He had rejuvenated worthless limbs, healed abandoned lepers, dismissed debilitating demons, and restored a blind man's sight. Surely He could — and certainly He would — come and heal their brother. After all, He was God. So Mary and Martha immediately sent an urgent message begging Him to come.

Jesus and His disciples were within walking distance of Bethany, but as close as He was to Mary and Martha (both in distance and friendship), He chose not to come to their rescue when they needed Him most. Lazarus died and was buried, and Jesus was nowhere to be seen. He had purposely chosen not to show up until it was too late!

John 11 describes the deep agony that Mary and Martha suffered at the loss of their brother and the anguish they felt at the absence of their friend. When Jesus finally got to Bethany, both sisters ran to him lamenting, "Lord, if you had been here, [our] brother would not have died" (verses 21,32). They knew that if their friend had chosen to intervene, this terrible tragedy would not have occurred.

But Jesus had a plan. He wanted to do something much more significant than heal a sick friend. It was only in Mary and Martha's bleakest moments of anguish and pain that Jesus was best able to demonstrate the full extent of God's power and the completeness of His love. It was in that time of great darkness that He could bring the greatest glory to God.

Jesus lovingly questioned Martha, "Did I not tell you that if you believed, you would see the glory of God?" (verse 40). He then proceeded to raise a four-day-old corpse from the grave in dramatic fashion. "Lazarus, come out!" He yelled — and, sure enough, Lazarus did! Can you imagine a fully wrapped mummy tromping its way out of a tomb in the middle of a graveyard in *real life* — not a movie?

God was not absent when Mary and Martha were experiencing extreme pain. He was implementing a plan. He didn't cause the illness that took Lazarus' life, but He used it to bring significant healing to many people who would otherwise have remained lost and dying. John 11:45 says, "Many of the Jews who had come to visit Mary, and had seen what Jesus did, put their faith in him."

No, God was not sleeping on the job, nor was He ignoring Mary and Martha's pain, and He certainly wasn't powerless to intervene. He was allowing suffering to achieve amazing results. If God can raise Lazarus from the dead, He can certainly handle whatever problems we are facing! Pain in our lives does not indicate God's absence, nor does it illustrate His weakness or inability or lack of care.

WE MUST ALLOW THE PAIN TO EMPOWER US — NOT IMPAIR US

Because of your involvement in athletics, you know exactly what I am referring to when I say that pain can empower. You have spent many hours in gyms working out and lifting weights. At times it has obviously been very painful. I've watched you grunt and groan and contort your faces as you've pumped and pushed and pulled various weights. Why on earth do you allow yourself to go through such agony? You do it because you understand that the more pain you are willing to endure in the weight room, the more power you will experience on the playing field.

Well, the same is true of the pain we suffer here on earth. It allows God's power to shine through us in ways that will have eternal results that we otherwise could not have experienced.

In his many years as a devoted follower of Christ, Paul became an expert in the school of adversity. But because he was able to face earthly trials with a heavenly perspective, he was able to maintain courage, hope, and joy. In 2 Corinthians 12:9-10 he says:

> Therefore I will boast all the more gladly about my weaknesses, so that Christ's power may rest on me. That is why, for Christ's sake, I delight in weaknesses, in insults, in hardships, in persecutions, in difficulties. For when I am weak, then I am strong.

Paul's response to pain and tragedy raised the curiosity of unbelievers all around him. As they saw the light of Christ shining through him, many were drawn to his Savior. In Philippians 2:14-16, Paul encouraged the believers, "Do everything without complaining or arguing, so that you may become blameless and pure, children of God without fault in a crooked and depraved generation, in which you shine like stars in the universe as you hold out the word of life."

I'm sure you're aware that the stars shine just as brightly during the day as they do at night. However, their light is insignificant compared to the brilliance of the sun. It is only when they are surrounded by darkness that the glittering stars can be counted in the sky. The same is true with our lives. The darker things are around us, the more our lives can shine.

Matthew 5:16 says, "Let your light shine before men, that they may see your good deeds and praise your Father in heaven." It's exciting to live in a time when the light from our lives can really make a difference.

You may have heard of the five missionary men who tried to bring the story of Jesus to the Auca Indians in Ecuador back in 1956 but were met with brutal hostility. They were speared to death on their first encounter with the natives. Their story is made remarkable by the fact that less than three years later, two of their wives returned to the same jungle tribe that had introduced horrible pain into their lives. They established contact with the very people who had murdered their husbands, and were personally able to share God's gospel of love with them. The sacrificial love and forgiveness of those women were bright beacons of light in the middle of dark hatred and fear. Through the power that came from their pain, a whole tribe of former warriors named "savages" by their head-hunting neighbors (Auca means "savage" in the Quechua language) is now serving God. Instead of choosing to stay home and mourn their loss, those two women chose to allow God's power to shine through them in a remarkable way.

WE MUST REMEMBER THAT OUR PAIN IS TEMPORARY

Our suffering is temporary even if it lasts a lifetime here on earth. Second Corinthians 4:17 says, "For our light and momentary troubles are achieving for us an eternal glory that far outweighs them all." Do you notice the adjectives Paul uses in this verse? He calls the troubles we are now going through *light* and *momentary* when compared to the *eternal* glory that far *outweighs* (okay, so that's a verb) them all! The size and duration of our present pain is nothing compared to the size and duration of the glory we'll experience in heaven. That eternal glory is described for us in Revelation 21:3-4, where we are told that God Himself will dwell with us in heaven and "He will wipe every tear from [our] eyes. There will be no more death or mourning or crying or pain."

We know where we are ultimately headed. We have a wonderful hope and expectation — one that people who don't know Christ cannot have. (I honestly don't know how they make it through the pain they encounter. They have no understanding that it can accomplish something meaningful in their lives or any prospect of it ever being eliminated.) First Peter 1:6-7 tells us that the trials we face will result in "praise, glory and honor" when we are with Jesus Christ. And the writer of Romans says, "I consider that our present sufferings are not worth comparing with the glory that will be revealed in us" (8:18).

I have no desire to change bodies with my wonderful friend Fred. To be cooped up by unresponsive muscles and unmanageable joints can't possibly be fun. Yet Fred allows God to use his damaged body to help with the singles ministry in our church. Can you imagine the glory and rejoicing there will be in heaven when Fred receives the perfect body God has designed for his eternal use? Wow! There is going to be dancing in heaven on that day — and Fred's going to be leading the conga line!

If pain is a place we have to go (and Jesus has told us it is, in John 16:33), then we should make the trip worthwhile. We should get everything out of it that we possibly can. We must accept it, learn from it, and let God use it! I'm not sure what Jonathan learned from his broken arm at age three (other than a little ambidexterity), but I do know that the rest of you (his brothers) learned a whole lot about being servants as you helped to feed him and tie his shoes. It drew us closer as a family. Remember, God always has a purpose for pain — or He wouldn't allow it!

SUMMARY

Painful experiences are inevitable because we live in a sinful world. But God always has a purpose for the pain that He permits to enter our lives. Sometimes God uses it to protect us, while other times He uses it to prune us. Through our pain, God can reveal His power, and often He uses it to spread the message of His love.

We must never mistake the presence of pain for the absence of God, nor should we infer from its existence that He is unable to deal with it. Although pain can impair us in some areas of our lives, we can let God use it to empower us in others. And we must keep in mind that our distress is temporary. There is a time coming when God will do away with all pain and suffering and we will live with Him for an eternity filled with His glory and joy. As we wait for the day when God will end all pain, suffering, and tears, we must hold tightly to the Word of God and let it shine through us in a dark and painful world. It is our job to attract others to a relationship with God that will allow them to spend their eternity free from sorrow and pain.

ISSUE #10

How Could God Possibly *Use* Me?

Thousands of people showed up on a hillside in Galilee to listen to the words of Jesus. As a long day of teaching drew to a close, the crowd of people who had followed Him into the remote countryside grew hungry. There were no nice restaurants or fast-food joints around — not even a 7-Eleven. And the closest town was miles away.

When Jesus asked His disciples to feed the crowd, they balked at the idea. Where would they get the food? Besides, to feed that many people would cost thousands of dollars! Philip estimated that it would cost at least eight months' wages feeding all the hungry people on that hillside (see John 6:7).

But God had a plan. He would perform a miracle to verify the fact that Jesus was His Son while demonstrating His awesome power and His loving provision. He would miraculously feed the five thousand men who were seated on the hillside, plus their wives and children!

God could have dropped manna from the heaven or flown in a whole flock of quail. That's how He chose to meet the needs of the Israelites when they grew hungry in the desert. He could have sent seagulls with bread in their beaks in the same way that He used ravens to feed Elijah when he was hiding from Queen Jezebel. He could have prompted a wonderful woman to load up a caravan of donkeys with home-cooked goodies and sent her to cater a huge dinner party like he had for David and his outlaw friends. But instead He chose to use the bag lunch of a little boy.

There was nothing unusual about that child. He was probably just an ordinary, freckle-faced kid who had tagged along with the crowd. And there was nothing spectacular about his lunch. It was just a few loaves of barley bread and two little fish that would satisfy his hunger until he could make it home for dinner. It was not anything more extraordinary than a peanut butter and jelly sandwich in a brown paper bag. But that ordinary little boy's very ordinary little lunch became extremely *extra*ordinary in the hands of the Messiah. Jesus multiplied the five loaves and two small fish into enough food to feed at least twelve thousand people, and there was so much left over that the disciples were able to fill twelve big baskets with the leftovers!

GOD USES ORDINARY PEOPLE TO DO EXTRAORDINARY THINGS

God has a habit of turning the regular into the remarkable. He takes great joy in transforming the common into the exceptional. Just think about the resumes of the disciples that He chose to accompany His Son. If you had been looking for leaders to head up a rapidly growing organization with a multicultural workforce and goals for international expansion, and you knew that the task would require great political savvy and include strong social opposition, would you have staked your future on a few common fishermen? After one glance you would have dumped most of the disciples' resumes in the office shredder. None of them had academic degrees or held important positions in society. They were not known for their wealth, and the majority of them had never traveled outside of their hometowns.

There are two things we can conclude about God's style of operating as we read through the Bible: (1) When God wants to do something extraordinary, He usually chooses to accomplish it through someone who is quite ordinary, and (2) He often uses methods that are very different from what we would expect.

- Noah was a farmer. He built an ark and became the father of the whole human race after the Great Flood.
- David was a shepherd. He killed a giant with his slingshot and became the king of Israel.
- Deborah was a mother. She led troops that did not have a single shield or spear to victory against an army that had nine hundred iron chariots.
- Paul was a Jewish scholar who liked to persecute the Christians. He took the message of Jesus Christ to the Gentiles and wrote many of the New Testament books.
- Mary was a simple peasant girl and Joseph was a carpenter. They raised the Son of God!

GIVE WHAT YOU HAVE TO GOD

There is only one condition that must be met before God will accomplish something completely astonishing through someone quite average — *that person must be willing to give what he or she has to God.* Do you understand the implications of that statement? God wants to do extraordinary things through you if you will let Him! All you have to do is be willing to give back to Him whatever He has already given you — whether it is miniscule or mammoth in the eyes of the world — and watch Him work!

Let's go back to the story of the hungry people on the hillside in Galilee. While they were milling around waiting for directions, Jesus asked His disciples to look for food. As Philip argued over the assignment, Andrew followed Christ's instructions. He located a kid with a bag lunch, and since no one else stepped forward to offer any other food, he brought the boy to Jesus.

"Here is a boy with five small barley loaves and two small fish," Andrew informed Jesus. "But how far will they go among so many?" (John 6:9). He obviously had reservations about the usefulness of his find. It was barely enough to satisfy the hunger of one growing boy. How could those few loaves and two little fish feed even one adult man?

But God did not require anything more than the availability of that little boy's lunch to carry out His plan. He never asks us to give Him anything we don't have, but He expects us to be willing to give up what we *do* have. And nothing is too trivial for His miraculous touch! There wasn't much in that little boy's bag to begin with, but when he gave what he had to Jesus, not only was there enough for everyone to eat, there were leftovers! Can you imagine that little boy trying to explain to his mother why there was still food in his lunch bag when he got home that night? ("Mama, how many fish did you put in there?")

Several years ago, Barbara Walters interviewed multibillionaire Ted Turner on the television program *20/20*. When she asked him what it was like to be so wealthy and successful, he replied that it was like holding an empty bag.[1]

Just think of all the things that Ted Turner has in his "bag"! He has broadcasting companies and sports teams and yachts and ski resorts, and there are probably a few small countries thrown in besides. He can buy any electronic gadget his heart desires and drive a different sports car every day of the week. Yet when he picks up the "bag" filled with all the things he owns in life, he says it feels empty. It doesn't satisfy him. Only God can give value to the things we own. And He will multiply that value beyond anything we can imagine if we will give our belongings to Him.

GIVE *ALL* THAT YOU HAVE TO GOD

Did you notice that the ordinary little boy with the ordinary little lunch willingly gave *all* that he had to God? I'm sure that he was starving just like everyone else on that hillside, but he didn't say, "Well, you know, I'm getting a little hungry myself. Maybe I should hang onto one or two of these loaves and bite off a piece of fish, but I'll gladly give the rest to you, Jesus." No, he gave it *all* to Jesus without knowing for sure whether he would get any back.

What has God placed in *your* "bag"? Have you given it all back to Him? Don't cling to anything — unless you don't want it to be blessed! That means giving God your friendships, your dating life, your relationship with your family, your athletic abilities, your musical talents, your schoolwork, your college goals, your future spouse, as well as all your stuff. It also means giving Him your time. Did you know that God multiplies time, too? If you take time to read the Bible and pray, God will give that time back to you in larger quantities than you would have had if you had not spent it with Him. I can testify to that!

At the beginning of this year I promised God that the first thing I would do every morning was read my Bible and pray. I wanted to make a habit of starting each day in His Word rather than trying to fit a quiet time with Him into my schedule whenever it was convenient. I bought a study guide that would help me read through the Bible in a year, and I was really enjoying spending at least half an hour with God every morning.

Then, just a few weeks ago, I realized that I was getting behind in my writing. I decided that I needed to finish Issue #7 *(Where Is God When I'm Afraid?)* that day because we were getting ready to leave town the very next day. I knew that I had several hours of work ahead of me to complete the chapter, and I also wanted to make it to Jonathan's baseball game later that afternoon. So I decided to skip my special morning quiet time with God and get straight to my typing. Since I do a lot of research in the Bible anyway, I figured that God would certainly understand my decision.

I spent most of that day searching for a Bible story that would illustrate the fact that when we fear God we don't need to fear anyone or anything else. After hours of study I finally came across exactly the right one! The passage was Exodus 1:15-21, the story I shared with you about the two Jewish midwives named Shiphrah and Puah. They dared to disobey the Pharaoh of Egypt because they feared God more than they feared him. Consequently, God blessed them by giving them children of their own. When I found this story, I was ecstatic, and immediately added it to the chapter.

As I left home for the ball game, I remember thinking how exciting it was that God had helped me find that story. I even mentioned to Dad that it was a good thing I had skipped my early morning quiet time, since I barely had time to finish the chapter.

Well, the next morning, when I opened my study guide, I realized that my assignment for the day before had been to read Exodus 1 and 2. I couldn't believe it! That was exactly the same passage I had spent most of the day trying to find! Instead of losing time, I would have gained three and a half hours if I had been willing to give my early morning time to God as I had promised Him I would! The time we spend with God in Bible study and prayer is so precious to Him that He will *always* bless us immeasurably and multiply it immensely when we give it to Him.

We should never try to measure anything we give to God by earthly mathematics or proportions. Divine blessings aren't limited by human logic or dimensions. Luke 6:38 tells us that if we give all that is in our "bags" to God, He will return them to us so full that extra stuff will fall out into our laps. It's impossible to outgive God.

GET READY TO BE SURPRISED BY GOD

We must never be embarrassed to give God what we have, no matter how small it is. As a matter of fact, the smaller the things and abilities we give to Him, the more we can see Him accomplish. Ken Davis tells a wonderful story in his book *I Don't Remember Dropping the Skunk But I Do Remember Trying to Breathe.* It's about a teenager named Ted.

> At fifteen, Ted Place gave his life to Jesus Christ. Because of the great sacrifice God had made for him, Ted wanted to give something back — but he felt he had nothing to give. He was the shortest kid in his class, he stuttered when he talked, and he had such a low self-esteem that he turned beet red whenever the teachers called on him.
>
> There was only one thing that Ted was really good at. He could turn somersaults better than anyone around. Since that was all he had to give, Ted gratefully gave it all to the Lord.
>
> The next day he went to the park to use this ability for God. In the middle of an open field, he began to turn somersaults. Soon a crowd of children gathered to watch. Impressed with his skill, they asked Ted how he had learned to tumble so

> well. He showed them how to do some simple tumbling tricks — and then, at the coaxing of the Holy Spirit, Ted took a deep breath and said, "I want to tell you something — I'm a Christian."
>
> Ted had expected that the kids would run away, or maybe laugh at him. Instead, a boy asked, "What do you mean you're a Christian?" Ted told them how he had given his life to Christ, and then he invited his new friends to church.
>
> Encouraged, the next day Ted went looking for more kids. Wherever he found a group of children, he would do somersaults and tumbling maneuvers and then tell the kids about the love of Jesus Christ.
>
> Ted didn't realize until many years later that God was doing a special miracle in his life. God had asked for the only skill Ted had: tumbling. When Ted was faithful in giving God his somersaults, God began to develop another talent Ted didn't even know he had. As he told hundreds of kids about the love of Christ, God was developing Ted's speaking ability. What started as a fifteen-year-old boy giving God his ability to do somersaults, snowballed into a full and exciting life of ministry that influenced the lives of thousands of people around the world . . . all because, at fifteen, he was willing to give God a gift that the world didn't value much.[2]

Ken Davis acknowledges that his own life was one of the many lives touched.

More often than not, what we have to offer will seem insignificant compared to the need at hand, but God plans it that way. He knows that what we have and what we can accomplish are nothing apart from His power. But He wants to surprise and thrill us with what *He* can do.

Imagine the feelings of inadequacy that little boy in Galilee must have had when he realized how many thousands of people needed to be fed by his lunch. Then picture the expression on his face as Jesus started tearing the bread and filling big baskets with the pieces. By the time the first little barley loaf was gone, his eyes must have been bugging out of his head! If you figure that one little boy was planning to eat two fish, how many fish do you think must have been handed out on the hillside that afternoon in order to feed those five thousand *men* — plus their wives and children? Jesus took the inadequate gift of that boy and multiplied it thousands of times.

Jonathan, do you remember when you first started to play the saxophone? Because we couldn't afford to buy you your own instrument, we borrowed one from the band instructor. All we needed to purchase was a new mouthpiece and the reeds to go in it. You brought that sax home every afternoon and practiced for what seemed like hours. It wasn't very long until we began to distinguish musical notes amid the squeaks and squawks.

But it was really amazing to hear the sounds that came from that same instrument when it was placed in the hands of your instructor. They were mellow and sweet and magnificent. No matter how well you played, he could always make the song sound better.

That's what happens when we give our talents and abilities and the things we own to God. No matter how inadequate we think they are, He can use them to do great things. And no matter how much we think we can accomplish with them on our own, He can accomplish more!

Think about how many spiritually hungry people there are in your life — friends who attend your school, kids who participate in sports activities with you, coworkers at your after-school job, neighbors who live down the street, and so on. What do you have in your "bag" that you can let God use to feed them?

I want to challenge you to give everything you have to God, no matter how valuable or useless it may seem to you. He will multiply it and use it to do extraordinary things. I guarantee that you will be surprised and thrilled by the results. He is an almighty God who wants to use YOU to accomplish unbelievable things. It doesn't matter how *ordinary* you are. It only matters how *available* you are!

SUMMARY

God often chooses to accomplish extraordinary things through ordinary people in ways that are different than we would expect. He chose to use an ordinary kid with an ordinary lunch to demonstrate His extraordinary power and loving provision to thousands of people on a hillside in Galilee. He takes great joy in transforming the regular into the remarkable. No matter how great or small our talents and possessions may be, He will multiply their value beyond anything we can imagine when we place them in His hands.

God wants us to give Him everything. That includes our friendships, our dating situations, our relationships with our families, our athletic abilities, our musical talents, our schoolwork, our college goals, and our future spouses, as well as our time and all of our stuff. He wants to surprise and thrill us with what He can do with them. He will use whatever we make available.

DISCUSSION QUESTIONS

ISSUE #1: SO, WHO AM I?

1. Read John 13:1-5.
    a. Why do you think none of the disciples offered to wash each other's feet?
    b. Why was Jesus willing to perform this lowly task?
2. Read John 1:12.
    a. How does someone become a child of God?
    b. How should being a child of God affect the way we live our lives? Why should it affect our lifestyle?
3. Name one aspect of your identity that you would like to change if you could. How does the fact that you are a child of God affect the way you view that identifying feature?
4. Read John 3:16 and 1 Peter 1:18-19. How much are you worth to God?
5. List five ways people search for security in life. (Several are mentioned in this chapter.) Beside each one explain why it is an unstable source of security.
6. Read Deuteronomy 33:27. Rewrite this verse in your own words for your own life situation emphasizing the security you have in God.

ISSUE #2: WHY AM I HERE?

1. How did God design for us to find true fulfillment and joy? How do most people try to find fulfillment and joy?

2. Read Galatians 1:10. In what ways is "pleasing men" different from "serving Christ"?
3. Read Ephesians 1:17-20. How does the Holy Spirit enable us to serve?
4. Can you think of a time when you had to choose between "pleasing men" and "serving Christ"? Which did you choose and what was the result?
5. Think of someone you know whose "feet need to be washed." How can you "wash" them this week?

ISSUE #3: WHAT IF THINGS FROM MY PAST HAVE MESSED UP MY FUTURE?

1. How does "scar tissue" grow in our lives?
2. What kind of damage does it cause?
3. Joseph named his sons Manasseh and Ephraim. Using the meanings of their names, explain how God wants us to deal with the hurts that come into our lives.
4. Read Luke 15:11-31.
   a. List five things you discover about the prodigal son.
   b. List five things you discover about the father.
5. Read Philippians 3:13-14. How does Paul deal with things from his past?
6. What do you need to "forget" from your past in order to press on to do great things for God?
7. Read Jeremiah 29:11. Rewrite it in your own words making it personal.

ISSUE #4: WHAT IF OTHERS MAKE FUN OF MY FAITH?

1. Read James 1:12.

   Think about someone competing in the Olympics.

a. Describe the various "trials" (tests) a young person must go through in order to win a medal.
b. What is the purpose of the medal?
c. How do you think the winner looks back on the "trials"?
d. What do you think James means when he tells us that God will give us a crown if we pass the test?

2. Read Psalm 23:4. Look very carefully at each word.
   a. Make five observations about our role in making it through trials. (This will take some thought.)
   b. Now make five observations about God's role in helping us go through them.
3. Describe a time you persevered through something difficult and found that the reward made the difficulty worthwhile.
4. Describe a time you were "persecuted" (teased or bullied) for your faith. If you cannot think of a time, what could that mean?
5. Read Romans 12:14. How should we react to those who "persecute" us for our faith? How can we do this?

ISSUE #5: IF I HAD WHAT THEY HAVE, I'D BE HAPPY TOO!

1. Watch thirty minutes of television or look through a magazine and write a brief description of five commercials or ads. How is each one designed to make you discontent?
2. Describe something you once longed for, but when you received it, you discovered it was not fulfilling.
3. Describe something you currently long for. Why do you think God has chosen not to give it to you at this time?
4. There are at least 2,350 verses in the Bible that talk about money and possessions. Why do you think there are so many? (There are only about 500 that deal with prayer!)

5. Read Matthew 6:19-21. How can we store treasures in heaven?

ISSUE #6: WHY DO I FEEL SO ANGRY SO OFTEN?

1. What are some physical and/or social factors that can prompt an angry reaction in teenagers?
2. What is the underlying cause of most anger?
3. Describe the last time you felt angry. Was it a selfish reaction? Were you expecting someone to supply happiness that only God can provide? Explain your answers.
4. Read James 1:19-20. What are some keys to avoiding anger?
5. Read Ephesians 4:26-27. How does anger give the devil a foothold?

ISSUE #7: WHERE IS GOD WHEN I'M AFRAID?

Divide a sheet of paper into five columns. You may want to turn your paper sideways to allow for more room to write.

1. In the first column, write down something that triggers fear in your life. For example, *My family is moving to a new city.*
2. In the second column list any *what-ifs* that are associated with this fear. For example, *What if no one likes me in my new school?*
3. In the third column define *what is*. Describe God's knowledge, power, and love as it relates to your situation. For example, *God knows that my family is planning to move; God is powerful enough to change my parents' minds if He wants to; God loves me enough to do what is best for me. Therefore, if we move I need to trust Him with the outcome.*
4. In the fourth column try to think of a person in the Bible who had to rely on God in a similar situation and summarize that person's story. For example, *Abraham had to move and God*

didn't even tell him where he was going (Genesis 12:1). You might want to call a pastor or youth leader to get other examples.

5. In the fifth column, write a short prayer that hands your fear over to God. For example, *God please take my fear of moving and make me excited about my new home and the new people I will meet. Please give me a very special new Christian friend by the time school starts—and, by the way, could you please help me make the basketball team? Thank you.*
6. Read Psalm 34:4 and write it across the top of your page.

ISSUE #8: WHY CAN LIFE BE SO DECENT ONE DAY, THEN SO DISCOURAGING THE NEXT?

1. Read Psalm 77:1-9.
   a. What kind of emotional condition does Asaph (the psalmist) seem to be in?
   b. What kind of physical condition does he seem to be in (see especially verse 4)?
   c. Although the psalm never identifies the specific problem Asaph is facing, what are some of the things he is struggling with?
2. Read Psalm 77:10-19.
   a. What causes the sudden shift in Asaph's outlook on life (see especially verse 11)?
   b. What specific event in the history of the nation Israel does Asaph seem to be describing in verses 15-19?

3. Read Psalm 77:20.
   a. In addition to looking at God and experiencing His power, what is another important step in defeating discouragement?
   b. Is there someone in your life who can help you make it through difficult times? (If so, sometime this week let that person know that you are grateful for his or her leadership and friendship. If not, pray that God will send you someone special.)
4. Reread verse 13.
   a. Do you think Asaph was still discouraged by the time he wrote this verse?
   b. Write down something very special that God has done in your life so that whenever you are discouraged you can look back at it and remember God's power and provision.

ISSUE #9: IF GOD LOVES ME, WHY DOES HE LET ME HURT?

1. What are four ways that God uses pain?
2. We learned that no one is exempt from pain. Describe a painful experience in your life (past or present). In what way do you think God has used (or is using) it?
3. How can God use pain to empower us?
4. Read Revelation 21. List five magnificent things we can look forward to in heaven.
5. What are you most looking forward to in heaven? Why?

ISSUE #10: HOW COULD GOD POSSIBLY USE *ME?*

1. List five things that are in the "bag" God has given you.
   a. Which of these things have you given back to God for Him to use however He wants to?
   b. How have you seen Him multiply and use it/them?

2. Is there something in your "bag" that you have difficulty giving to God? Why is it hard to give it to Him?
3. Read Luke 18:18-24.
   a. What did the ruler want Jesus to give him?
   b. What did he not want to give to Jesus?
   c. Why do you think he wanted to hang onto the things in his "bag"?
4. Think about the time you spend with God each day.
   a. How do you spend this time with God?
   b. Does this amount of time indicate how much you love and trust Him? Why or why not?
   c. Do you need to spend more time with Him? If so, when will you do this?
5. Think about some of the spiritually hungry people in your life. Write down the name of at least one of them who you will pray for every day. What talent or gift has God given you that He could use to draw that person closer to relationship with Himself?
6. Read Zephaniah 3:17. List five things it teaches you about your relationship with God.

NOTES

ISSUE #1: SO, WHO AM I?

1. The Klondike Weekly. *American Heroes of the Klondike Gold Rush*. On-line source. *http://www.yukonalaska.com/klondike/bystate.html*. May 1, 1998.
2. McFarland, Ginger E. "Beyond Beauty." *Today's Christian Woman*. On-line source. *http://www.christianitytoday.com/tcw/9w4/9w4024.html*. July/Aug 1999.

ISSUE #2: WHY AM I HERE?

1. Technisch Instituut Sint-Vincentius. *Mother Teresa: The Official Website*. On-line source. *http://www.tisv.be/mt/life.htm*. April 4, 2000.
2. In Touch Ministries. *Portraits of Great Christians: Amy Carmichael, The Abandoned Life*. On-line source. *http://www.intouch.org/myintouch/mighty/portraits/*. Copyright 2002.
3. In Touch Ministries.

ISSUE #3: WHAT IF THINGS FROM MY PAST HAVE MESSED UP MY FUTURE?

1. Dawson McAllister, *Please Don't Tell My Parents: Answers for Kids in Crises* (Dallas: Word Publishing, 1992), p. 154.

ISSUE #6: WHY DO I FEEL SO ANGRY SO OFTEN?

1. James V. O'Connor, "Why Are We So #!&*@ MAD?" *USA Today.* Sept. 2000. On-line source <*http://www.findarticles.com/cf/0/m1272/2664129/65230213/print.jhtml*> 01/04/2002.
2. Patrick Morley, *The Man in the Mirror* (Grand Rapids, Mich.: Zondervan, 1999), p. 274.

ISSUE #7: WHERE IS GOD WHEN I'M AFRAID?

1. Warren Wiersbe, "Devotions for Your Spiritual Journey." Back to the Bible. On-line source <*http://www.backtothebible.org/devotions/features/year/27*> 1-18-02.

ISSUE #10: HOW COULD GOD POSSIBLY USE *ME*?

1. Bradford W. Swift, "Transforming the Golden Ghetto." *Life on Purpose.* On-line source <*http://www.lifeonpurpose.com/Project%20Purpose/transformingthegolden.html.* Copyright 1998. 3/20/02.
2. Ken Davis, *I Don't Remember Dropping the Skunk But I Do Remember Trying to Breathe* (Grand Rapids, Mich.: Zondervan, 1990), pp. 20-21. Used with author's permission.

ABOUT THE AUTHOR

GWENDOLYN MITCHELL DIAZ began life as a missionary kid in Nigeria, but moved to the United States at age ten. A graduate of the University of Pennsylvania, she spent many years working in the medical profession and writing articles and columns about sports, family, and her faith in God. She also has published the books *The Adventures of Mighty Mom, Mighty Mom's Secrets for Raising Super Kids, Sticking Up for What I Believe* (NavPress), and *Sticking Up for What Is Right* (NavPress).

As a mother of four boys, Gwen feels particularly passionate about helping teens solidify their faith and grow as Christians. Her goal is to present God's love to them in a way that will transform their lives. In *Sticking Up for Who I Am* she defines a teenager's value in light of that love. She and her husband, Ed, seek to convey God's truths to teens in terms they can understand and embrace and enjoy!

ABOUT THE AUTHOR

[illegible]